Dramaturgy and History

Dramaturgy and History provides a practical account of an aspect of dramaturgical practice that is often taken for granted: dramaturgs' engagements with history and historiography. Dramaturgs play a vital role in amplifying and activating theatre's unique potential to contribute to the pressing public discourse around the uses and legacies of history. This collection challenges the notion of history as an unassailable or settled set of facts, offering readers a glimpse into the processes and methods of eighteen dramaturgs working in a variety of settings, including professional theatres, universities, museums, and archives. The dramaturgs featured use history to a variety of ends: they reframe classical texts for contemporary audiences; advocate for the production of lesser-known writers and the expansion of the canon; create new works that bring women's, LGBTQIA+, and Global Majority histories to life; and establish new and necessary archives by/of/for minoritarian artists. Collectively, they examine and animate some of the most urgent questions, concerns, and challenges that dramaturgs encounter in working with history. An essential resource for teachers and students of dramaturgy, the collection offers a concluding hands-on exercise for each chapter to facilitate the reader's application of the methods discussed in their own practice.

Caitlin A. Kane (they/she) is an Assistant Professor of Theatre History and Dramatic Criticism at Kent State University.

Erin Stoneking (she/her) is an Assistant Professor in the Department of Gender and Race Studies at The University of Alabama.

Focus on Dramaturgy
Series Editor: Magda Romanska

The *Focus on Dramaturgy* series from Routledge – developed in collaboration with TheTheatreTimes.com – is devoted to the craft of dramaturgy from multiple contemporary perspectives. This groundbreaking comprehensive series is authored by top professionals in the field, addressing a variety of current hot topics in dramaturgy.
The series is edited by Magda Romanska, an author of the critically-acclaimed *Routledge Companion to Dramaturgy*, dramaturg, writer, theatre scholar, and Editor-in-Chief of TheTheatreTimes.com.

Dramaturgy of Form
Performing Verse in Contemporary Theatre
Kasia Lech

The Dramaturgy of History
Tom Bryant

Dramaturgy of Sex on Stage in Contemporary Theatre
Edited by Kate Mulley

The Dramaturgy of Performing Science
New Work in Interdisciplinary Contexts
Jules Odendahl-James

New Dramaturgies of Contemporary Opera
The Practitioners' Perspectives
Edited by Jingyi Zhang

Dramaturgy and History
Staging the Archive
Edited by Caitlin A. Kane and Erin Stoneking

For more information about this series, please visit: https://www.routledge.com/performance/series/RFOD

Dramaturgy and History

Staging the Archive

Edited by
Caitlin A. Kane and Erin Stoneking

LONDON AND NEW YORK

First published 2025
by Routledge
4 Park Square, Milton Park, Abingdon, Oxon OX14 4RN

and by Routledge
605 Third Avenue, New York, NY 10158

Routledge is an imprint of the Taylor & Francis Group, an informa business

British Library Cataloguing-in-Publication Data
A catalogue record for this book is available from the British Library

ISBN: 9781032636283 (hbk)
ISBN: 9781032636290 (pbk)
ISBN: 9781032636337 (ebk)

DOI: 10.4324/9781032636337

Typeset in Times New Roman
by codeMantra

C.K.: To Silas, Parsnip, and Rosemary
E.S.: To Matt and Louisa

Contents

Contributors

Ryan Adelsheim (they/them) is a new play dramaturg, producer, and lecturer at Tufts University, Medford, MA. Their writing has appeared in *Theater* where they co-edited the special issue "Expanding Devised Theater" (54:2). They are a doctoral candidate at Yale Drama, where their research focuses on queer and trans theater and performance.

Elaigwu P. Ameh (he/him) is the Karen Peterson Wilson Assistant Professor of Theater at St. Olaf College, Northfield, MN. His current book projects are *Lives Between the Lines: Performing Internal Displacement in Nigeria* and *Performing Black Fatherhood: Fabrication, Silence, Repair*. He is the dramaturg for Theatre for Concerted Change (T4CC).

Nicole Anderson Cobb (she/her) is an American historian, playwright, and researcher. Her work has been featured in local, regional, and national publications including The Story with Dick Gordon (APM), WGLT, WBEZ, *The Reader*, *The Chicago Sun-Times, The News Gazette, The Lutheran Magazine*, *Smile Politely Magazine*, and Sixty Inches from Center.

Laurie Arnold (Sinixt Band Colville Confederated Tribes) (she/her/tkəɬmilxʷ) is Professor of History and Director of Native American Studies at Gonzaga University, Spokane, WA. Her scholarship includes US federal Indian policy and contemporary Native American drama and has been published in *the Western Historical Quarterly* and *The Public Historian.* The University of Washington Press published her monograph.

Lindsay L. Barr (she/her) is a freelance dramaturg and arts administrator. A graduate of Carnegie Mellon University with a degree focus in dramaturgy, she is now based in Pittsburgh, PA. Lindsay is an active member of Literary Managers and Dramaturgs of the Americas and board member for Bay area-based Aviva Arts.

Al Evangelista (he/siya) is an Assistant Professor of Dance at Oberlin College, Oberlin, OH. Al's work focuses on the intersections of dance and culture, particularly in queer Filipinx-American narratives. His most recent projects were incubated in a Dancing Lab at the National Center for Choreography at The University of Akron.

Percival Hornak (he/him) received his MFA in Dramaturgy and Certificate in Feminist Scholarship from the University of Massachusetts Amherst, Amherst, MA, in 2023. He co-produces the podcast *Dungeons + Drama Nerds* and proudly serves as Literary Manager of Stroller Scene, a new play advocacy organization based in New York City.

Caitlin A. Kane (they/she) is an Assistant Professor of Theatre History at Kent State University, Kent, OH. As an artist-scholar, Kane's research centers on feminist and queer approaches to staging history. Their scholarship has been published in *Theatre Topics*, *The Journal of American Drama and Theatre*, and *The Scholar as Human.*

Khalid Y. Long (he/him) is an Associate Professor of Theatre Arts at Howard University, Washington, DC. He is the co-editor of *Contemporary Black Theatre and Performance: Acts of Rebellion, Activism, and Solidarity*. A scholar-dramaturg-pedagogue, Long's work addresses the intersections of race, class, gender, and sexuality within marginalized and oppressed communities.

Alison Hyde Pascale (she/her) is a doctoral student in the Theatre and Performance program at The Graduate Center, City University of New York, New York, NY. Her research encompasses the interrelationship between theatre and religion, focusing on plays written by nuns in the Medieval and Early Modern period and alternative religious movements of the twentieth and twenty-first centuries.

Charlie Peters (ze/hir/hirs) is a lifelong resident of Treaty 6 territory in what is colonially known as Canada. Hir scholarly work has been published in *Canadian Theatre Review*, *Theatre Research in Canada, Comedy Studies*, *Howlround*, and *The Canadian Theatre Encyclopedia*. www.charliepeters.ca

Jennifer Popple (she/her) is an Associate Professor of Theatre at Augustana College, Rock Island, IL. She has published books, articles, and reviews on the English Restoration actress, eighteenth-century theatre, and Paula Vogel. Recent directing credits include William Shakespeare's *Macbeth*, Sarah Ruhl's *In the Next Room*, and Sophie Treadwell's *Machinal.*

Sam Redway (he/him) is a dramaturg, community animateur, and previously Junior Fellow at Guildhall School of Music and Drama, London, UK. He co-wrote *Bin Laden: The One Man Show* (Knaïve Theatre), wrote *The Girl with a Hurricane Brain* (dir. Katie Mitchell), and is Associate Artist of Smoking Apples Theatre Company.

Elysia Segal (she/her) is Producer of Public Programs at the Intrepid Museum in New York City and served as Project Director of their Crossing the Line outreach program. She is currently President of the International Museum Theatre Alliance, certified through the National Association for Interpretation, and is a NASA (National Aeronautics and Space Administration) Solar System Ambassador.

Janna Segal (she/her) is an Associate Professor of Theatre Arts at the University of Louisville, Louisville, KY. Her research has appeared in anthologies and in *Review*, *SDC Journal*, *JEMCS*, and *Shakespeare.* With Idris Goodwin, she co-adapted *I Know Why the Caged Bird Sings.* She is the Comparative Drama Conference's dramaturg.

Daphnie Sicre (she/her/ella) is an Assistant Professor at the University of California Riverside, Riverside, CA. Among other publications, she contributed to *Black Acting Methods*, *The Routledge Companion to Latine Theatre and Performance*, and *Contemporary Black Theatre and Performance*. She was resident dramaturg at The Robey Theatre and is now Co-Artistic Director at Ammunition Theatre.

Erin Stoneking (she/her) is an Assistant Professor in the Department of Gender and Race Studies at The University of Alabama, Tuscaloosa, AL. Her writing has appeared in *Response: The Journal of Popular and American Culture* and *Theatre Journal*. She is dramaturg and co-writer for *The Moods of Dotts Johnson in Song*.

Ilinca Tamara Todoruţ (she/her) is Assistant Professor of Theatre at Babeş-Bolyai University, Cluj-Napoca, Romania, and author of *Christoph Schlingensief's Realist Theater* (2021). She contributed to *The Routledge Companion to Dramaturgy* (2015) and published articles in journals such as *Theater*, *TDR*, *Performance Research*, and *Theatre History Studies*.

Yiwen Wu (she/her) is a PhD student in Theater and Performance Studies and East Asian Languages and Civilizations at the University of Chicago, Chicago, IL. Her credits include *The Chinese Lady* and *The Feet of God* at Timeline Theater, *Hungry Ghost Festival* at Lifeline Theater, and *Lucy & Charlie's Honeymoon* at Lookingglass Theatre.

Acknowledgments

From the beginning of this project, J. Ellen Gainor and Sara Warner have been tireless advocates for our work and generous mentors. We are similarly indebted to the scholars and artists who participated in the sessions we organized on dramaturgy, performance, and history through Cornell University, the American Society for Theatre Research, the Association for Theatre in Higher Education, and the National Council on Public History. Completion of this project was supported by The University of Alabama's College of Arts and Sciences and Department of Gender and Race Studies and Kent State University's Office of Student Research. This book would not have been possible without the perseverance and perspicacity of our contributors and the editorial support of our research assistants, Virgo Denning and Harmony Leverett. Finally, we would like to thank Magda Romanska, Claire Margerison, Steph Hines, and Swatti Hindwan at Routledge for championing and supporting this project.

Introduction

Caitlin A. Kane and Erin Stoneking

Mark Bly has memorably described the defining act of the dramaturg as inquiry: "I question" (49). The roots of the word "history," likewise, emphasize not just passive knowledge of past events but knowledge acquired through the act of inquiry, a search for information driven by an abiding curiosity. This sense of the word draws attention to the often unacknowledged processes of researching and writing history, belying the common notion that history is an incontestable, complete, and impartial view into the past. Similarly, Bly's pithy response to the oft-asked question of what a dramaturg does disrupts popular misconceptions about dramaturgs as fonts of otherwise static knowledge: the dramaturg does not simply relay predetermined answers but plays a dynamic role in the creative process.

In the spirit of Bly's conception of dramaturgy (and our own), this volume seeks a fuller account of one aspect of dramaturgy that is often taken for granted: dramaturgs' engagement with and application of historical research. To say that dramaturgs regularly undertake historical research and grapple with questions about how to present or contextualize histories for contemporary artists and audiences might seem to be stating the obvious. Indeed, introductory dramaturgy manuals unfailingly list broad familiarity with theatre history and cultural history and the ability to research and write historical contexts and production histories as crucial skills for effective dramaturgs. Michael Mark Chemers, for example, notes that "historical research is the bread-and-butter of dramaturgy that provides the basis of understanding that any production needs to succeed" (45). Researching and providing historical context is "one of the most salient dramaturgical practices," writes Magda Romanska, part of dramaturgy "since the beginning of the profession" (10).[1] At the same time, these manuals caution against the impulse to embrace the authority of historical research so entirely that the dramaturg alienates their collaborators or becomes an impediment to a dynamic production process. Instead, dramaturgs must develop an ineffable sensibility allowing them to discern when and how historical information might expand creative and receptive processes.

DOI: 10.4324/9781032636337-1

Many introductory handbooks and anthologies include excellent case studies illustrating the application of historical research to production. Robert Scanlan, for example, demonstrates the fundamental shifts in interpretation of Gotthold Ephraim Lessing's *Minna von Barnhelm* that occur when one takes into account Lessing's biography and eighteenth-century German military history (93–7). Cary M. Mazer and Susan Jonas, through an array of productions, outline philosophies and methods for assessing what histories will best assist dramaturgs and directors to "acknowledge, if not to bridge" the difference between historical and contemporary cultures (Mazer 294) or to create, from canonical texts, productions "*about* that difference" (Jonas 245). Yet these case studies represent relatively brief segments in volumes that encompass dramaturgical practice more broadly. Practical guidebooks—particularly those which aim to treat the breadth of dramaturgical methods and contexts—are necessarily constrained in their ability to delve into the technicalities of historical research and its applications. This is even more the case for guidebooks intended for student and early career dramaturgs, where—given the fluid nature of dramaturgy, and despite its growing recognition and institutionalization—a considerable amount of space must be devoted to limning and historicizing the field itself. Certainly, dramaturgical practices, needs, and settings vary widely, and dramaturgs must be responsive to specific collaborations. Though introductory manuals may offer general guidelines and norms, they are, befittingly, careful to note that no one protocol for generating and activating historical context will apply in all situations. As a result, coverage of dramaturgs' engagement with history as a discrete skill set or function can feel somewhat diffuse or abstract. Practicing dramaturgs may feel the importance of historical research and context to dramaturgical work is self-evident, but asserting history's significance to dramaturgical practice without providing adequate demonstration of that fact may risk inadvertently reinforcing the worst and most prevalent misconceptions about dramaturgy: that it is an academic exercise peripheral to creative and collaborative processes. The essays included in this collection illustrate that, far from being incidental to the production process, dramaturgy—and the historical research that is often at its core—play an essential role in developing engaging performance.

Just as dramaturgy has sometimes been treated as ancillary rather than integral to the creative process, popular understandings of history have long cast the word into the realm of the capitalized and therefore unapproachable: "History"—an established field of knowledge disconnected from most people's day-to-day lives. However, recent increased public engagement with debates over history, national identity, and collective memory in the United States and abroad suggests a growing awareness of the impact of historical narratives on contemporary issues. Re-examinations of accepted histories and attention to historiographical questions have captured the public imagination, with particular emphasis on how history might help us navigate and understand our present. For instance, in August 2019, journalist Nikole Hannah-Jones published *The*

1619 Project, in which she explored the longstanding and far-reaching legacies of the institution of slavery in the United States. The project centered slavery as a defining factor in American history and argued that it continues to inform the policies and systems that shape the lives of Americans today. In the intervening years, *The 1619 Project* has become a flashpoint in burgeoning debates over the purpose, interpretation, and uses of history, which have become entwined with broader political and ideological conflicts. Where critics saw the project as an effort to reshape the narrative of American history, its supporters celebrated it as an overdue intervention in dominant and exclusionary interpretations of the United States's past. How is history told? Who gets to tell it? How are the legacies of the past understood to shape our experiences and institutions in the current moment? This contestation of history's significance and narration has crystallized in several other arenas of public life, including debates over history curricula, the removal of Confederate monuments, and the interpretation of the US Constitution in recent Supreme Court rulings. At the heart of these debates is a sense of urgency regarding history's bearing on the present: history, those on all sides of the debate implicitly understand, guides how we understand ourselves and how we understand and respond to the complexities of our contemporary moment.

The public's investment in these debates demonstrates that, far from being staid, distant, or irrefutable, history is dynamic, polyvocal, and urgent and merits our ongoing engagement. History is not a monolithic or neutral entity. The artifacts that serve as historical evidence are only fragments of the expanse of historical human experience. The institutional archives from which histories are often crafted are ideologically inflected and have historically been curated by individuals who have been granted the epistemic and sociopolitical power to determine whose histories are worthy of preservation. Moreover, the work of historiography—identifying archival materials, interpreting them, and crafting a narrative of the past—is necessarily shaped by the particular subjectivity, identities, conceptual frameworks, and temporal location of the historian undertaking it. As such, the work of historiography is always a political enterprise. Therefore, we must acknowledge that history is always incomplete: mainstream historical narratives and collecting practices have been the instruments of marginalization and exclusion, and have served to legitimize violence and injustice. There is, emphatically, value in calling attention to and intervening in such silences and erasures to redress them. Yet, the past ultimately evades total apprehension: even as we undertake the vital work of better and more fully understanding it, we must grapple with the reality that our capacity to recover the past is limited.

Live theatre's ability to imaginatively animate the past—to bring historical figures and events into physical and temporal relation to us via the stage—positions it as an important medium for amplifying and responding to history's complex and contested resonances in the present. At the theatre, we collectively witness co-present, living bodies realizing, synchronically with our own durational time, action on a human scale. History-based theatre upends the notion that history is a remote or settled set of objective facts. New productions of historical works call on us to recognize and re-examine the values and beliefs of the eras in which they were written, reinterpreting them —whether to render them comprehensible for contemporary audiences or to challenge their validity by introducing analysis informed by present-day thought. Dramaturgs, in their synonymousness with mediation and "betweenness" (Proehl 136), play a crucial role in activating and mining the intersection between history and theatre. This is perhaps best encapsulated in the oft-repeated foundational question of dramaturgical practice: "Why this play now?" As the question suggests, the dramaturg is principally concerned not with an exacting recreation of "this play" in its original historical context, nor with an exhaustive recounting of the history dramatized by "this play," but with forging a meaningful connection between this play (including the multiple histories that inform it) and the artists and audiences who collectively breathe life into it. The work of the dramaturg frequently overlaps with the work of the historian, seeking out traces of the past in archives and libraries, and working to analyze those traces and communicate accounts of the past. Rather than take this overlap for granted, we contend that closer attention to the intersection of dramaturgical and historical research illuminates the theatre's unique capacity to respond to ongoing debates regarding the uses and legacies of history.

It is necessary to note that just because theatre can foreground and engage with the contested, political, and incomplete nature of history does not mean that "staging the archive" invariably results in critical interrogations of history and its production. Theatre can and has been used to fortify and disseminate prevailing ideas about history as a grand, unassailable, linear narrative; it has also reproduced the familiar dimensions of dominant, exclusionary, and colonial histories. However, it is theatre's potential to contribute meaningfully and uniquely to the pressing discourse around history and historiography, taken together with our understanding of the role of the dramaturg not as accuracy monitor but as inquiring mediator and collaborator, that we wish to foreground in this collection. To that end, we have privileged work that intervenes in existing historical narratives and that critically animates histories that have too often been left out of them. We have sought out dramaturgs who, in their work, are grappling with the problems of historiography.

The eighteen contributors—dramaturgs working in professional theatres, academic institutions, and community organizations—offer readers brief case studies that provide vital insights into the critical and illuminating ways that dramaturgs put history to use. The case study format allows each author to ground the methods they outline in practice and yields a concrete view of the processes of dramaturgs at work. The array of case studies included speaks to the breadth of dynamic circumstances under which dramaturgs employ historical research and historical thinking and demonstrates the diversity of dramaturgical approaches available. The dramaturgs featured in this collection use history to a variety of ends: they reframe classical texts for contemporary audiences; advocate for the production of lesser-known writers and the expansion of the canon; create new works that bring women's, LGBTQIA+, and Global Majority histories to life; and establish new and necessary archives by/of/for minoritarian artists who have too-long been overlooked. Collectively, they examine and animate some of the most urgent questions, concerns, and challenges that dramaturgs encounter in working with history. How can dramaturgs most effectively identify, select, and synthesize historical materials that meet the needs of a particular production? What are the dramaturg's ethical responsibilities when engaging with and summarizing histories for the creative team and audience, particularly given these histories' inextricability from colonialism, racism, and cis-heteropatriarchy? How can dramaturgical skills be repurposed for extra-theatrical contexts including schools, historical sites, museums, and archives?

We envision this volume as a practical handbook that offers avenues by which readers (especially students and emerging artists) can forge their own answers to these questions. In the interest of providing the reader a broad orientation to the dramaturgical working contexts covered, the collection is divided into three sections:

I Production Dramaturgy: (Re)contextualizing Existing Plays
II New Play Development: Staging History and Historiography
III Dramaturgy and/as Public History: Connecting with Broader Publics

We hope that this organizational framework will facilitate the usability of the text; however, we do not wish to suggest that these modes of dramaturgical practice exist in isolation from one another. We encourage readers to productively read across sections if they are interested in particular historiographic or theoretical concerns. The collection's organization into familiar stages of dramaturgical involvement also enables readers to identify chapters that can be used to address the specific challenges encountered in their practice. To further facilitate application of the practices outlined in the collection, each chapter concludes with an exercise that encapsulates one key aspect of the author's methodology. These exercises invite readers to think differently about historical research, focusing not only on sharing historically accurate information but also on creating contexts in which we can all engage critically and imaginatively with complex, multifaceted histories; their resonances in the present; and the potentialities they open up for the future.

Production Dramaturgy: (Re)contextualizing Existing Plays

In the course of supporting productions of existing history-based or historical works of drama, the seven dramaturgs featured in this section demonstrate that the production dramaturg is more than the fusty arbiter of historical authenticity. What methods do dramaturgs employ to render histories and historic works meaningful and vivid to contemporary audiences and artists? What historical contexts (and modes of presenting this context) best prepare artists and audiences to meet historical or history-based plays? What approaches can dramaturgs take to collaborate with artists and audiences in interrogating and redressing problematic elements of historical works?

Khalid Y. Long, Jennifer Popple, and Charlie Peters reframe and revitalize canonical works by frequently produced playwrights, providing new emphases and conceptual foundations for contemporary artists and audiences. Long's chapter illustrates how race-conscious conceptual casting—beyond the benefits of inclusion—can generatively shape production dramaturgy, allowing productions to explore perspectives and histories marginalized in or absent from the original text. Long turns to the history of the Great Migration, anti-miscegenation laws, and queer spaces in St. Louis to develop and enrich a production concept for Tennessee Williams's *The Glass Menagerie* (1944) with a multiracial cast. Popple offers an approach to foregrounding and challenging outmoded biases in canonical works without altering the play's script. Building on the standard dramaturgical tools of script analysis and historical and theoretical research, Popple details a system for surfacing the gendered and racialized power dynamics at play in Arthur Miller's *The Crucible* (1953). Peters argues for the importance of connecting productions with local histories in audience engagement efforts, even when the play itself is set elsewhere. Peters emphasizes, in hir account of creating a lobby display for a Canadian production of Bertolt Brecht's 1941 *The Resistible Rise of Arturo Ui* (*Der aufhaltsame Aufstieg des Arturo Ui*), the decolonizing potential of considering a play's resonances with local historical contexts.

Championing less familiar works, Alison Hyde Pascale and Janna Segal animate plays written by women and often relegated to the status of static historical artifacts rather than versatile scripts. In their case studies, Pascale and Segal exemplify production dramaturgy's vital role in challenging such notions and expanding the canon. Confronting the tendency, among Early Modern productions, to reserve contemporizing concepts for Shakespeare's putatively "universal" oeuvre, Pascale recounts her dramaturgical support for a production of Sor Juana Inés de la Cruz's 1683 *House of Desires (Los Empeños de Una Casa)* re-envisioned in a contemporary Mexican resort hotel. Pascale leverages translation as a metaphor and practical exercise to encourage the cast and audiences to consider the play a dynamic entity. Janna Segal takes up Jane Barnette's concept of adapturgy to offer dramaturgical methods for adapting neglected historical works for contemporary audiences and online-only production formats. Using social media, identity-conscious casting, and the creation of a new character who represents a historically grounded counterforce to the original play's racist elements, Janna Segal acts as both production dramaturg and co-adapter in creating a virtual and updated production of Anna Cora Mowatt's *Fashion* (1845), here titled *[Re]Fashion.*

Yiwen Wu and Percival Hornak both provide production dramaturgy for contemporary plays that dramatize historical material, concomitantly emphasizing theatre's potential to address historiographical challenges such as archival absences and changing identity categories. Wu demonstrates how a production dramaturg can amplify a play's structural investment in historical thinking in ways that shape both staging choices and audience engagement. Wu's dramaturgy contributed to the development of a metatheatrical frame for a production of Lloyd Suh's *The Chinese Lady* (2018), underscoring the play's critique of historical and contemporary Orientalist gazes. Hornak proposes a queer historiographic approach to production dramaturgy for plays that deal with queer histories. Hornak's method, illustrated via a production of Sarah Ruhl's *Orlando* (2010), intervenes in dominant and exclusionary historical narratives of LGBTQIA+ lives by attending to the personal and affective resonances and imaginative sparks that affirm a transhistorical queer community.

New Work Dramaturgy: Staging History and Historiography

The six case studies in this section examine how artists transform historical research into dramatic representations of historical narratives and the historiographic process. Many of the new works featured engage critically and creatively with the personal, cultural, and ethical dilemmas associated with the writing of minoritarian histories. They remind us that writing history is not a neutral process and that the rendering of history into dramatic form is a political act. These chapters invite us to consider what strategies allow dramaturgs and their collaborators to compellingly frame, structure, and dramatize historical events for contemporary audiences. How can artists ethically represent histories that have been imperfectly and incompletely recorded in the archive? What methods aid us in balancing the optimistic desire to recover or repair minoritarian histories with the reality that many of the archives we work with have been shaped by histories of structural oppression and violence?

Ryan Adelsheim, Al Evangelista, and Erin Stoneking's chapters address creating new works from fragmented and incomplete archives of historically marginalized groups. Together, they offer readers tools for using performance to illuminate the historiographic process: the process by which history has been written (and, sometimes, *failed* to be written). Adelsheim discusses the development of Emil Weinstein's *soldiergirls*, a musical comedy about lesbian relationships in the Women's Army Corps during the 1940s. Adelsheim describes a queer dramaturgical approach that strategically employs anachronism, camp, and collage to foreground the resonances between the historical protagonists' lived experiences and those of contemporary LGBTQIA+ individuals, including the members of the creative team. In so doing, *soldiergirls* eschews strict adherence to sometimes scant historical evidence, creating a more complex portrayal of the risks and joys associated with the women's love. Evangelista details his approach to creating *somewhere good*, a dance performance that uses augmented reality to unpack the inhumane treatment of Filipinx participants in the 1904 St. Louis World Fair's "human zoo." Rather than attempting to repair the gaps in the archival record, which includes no testimony from the individuals who were on display, Evangelista uses fragmentation in the dancers' movement, the sound design, and the augmented reality text to draw the audience's attention to the impossibilities of recovering minoritarian histories and to the difficult necessity of grappling with the persistence of anti-Asian hate and colonial violence. Taking up another incomplete archive, Stoneking elucidates how the writing and dramatizing of history became co-constitutive processes when a group of artist-scholars came together to research the life of Dotts Johnson, a mid-twentieth-century African American performing artist whose life and career have gone largely unstudied until this team, led by his granddaughter Luvada A. Harrison, set out to write a musical about his life. By establishing "animating loss" as a dramaturgical principle for the musical, Stoneking offers readers a model for managing simultaneous research and developmental processes that productively inform one another.

Elaigwu P. Ameh, Lindsay L. Barr, and Sam Redway's chapters center on collaborative dramaturgical processes used to create new plays with groups of relatively amateur artists about histories relevant to their lives. These authors were tasked with not only supporting the crafting of the plays on which they worked but also managing the historical data used in their creation and facilitating significant portions of the collaborative processes through which they were realized. In Ameh's chapter about gathering the stories of internally displaced persons in a refugee camp in Nigeria and devising his play *Displaced* with them, Ameh demonstrates that dramaturgs can use ethnographic methods to mitigate some of the ethical challenges that accompany telling the stories of disempowered groups. He suggests that the key to this approach is centering those individuals' artistic and political impulses. In her discussion of the development and production of Liza Birkenmeier's *The Way Out West*, Barr explores how de-centered and collaborative approaches to dramaturgy that involve all members of the artistic team can result in particularly nuanced storytelling and a more fruitful development period for playwrights. Collaborative dramaturgy, she argues, requires the dramaturg to embrace the roles of facilitator, communicator, and record-keeper as they empower actors and designers to take ownership of the dramaturgical work inherent to their artistic practices. Part historical reenactment, part community-based play, *The Macclesfield Potato Riot of 1812* was developed by Redway with residents of Macclesfield, UK. In his account of this developmental process, Redway describes a method for tracking the temporal relationships between the past and the present that allows creators to identify key moments of historical resonance and facilitates more effective collaboration amongst large and transient groups of participants.

Dramaturgy and/as Public History: Connecting with Broader Publics

This section features five case studies in which dramaturgs and public historians engage in work that is dramaturgically minded and invested in performance practice, though frequently in settings that are not always recognizably theatrical. Each of these chapters is driven by desires shared with the field of public history: to engage broader publics in historical research and interpretation, to yield greater access to histories, and to build meaningful collaborative relationships with stakeholders in those histories. How can theatre artists and (public) historians work together to invite engagement in/with diverse and critical histories? What might thinking more expansively about what counts as dramaturgical practice open up for us as a field?

Elysia Segal, Ilinca Tamara Todoruţ, and Nicole Anderson Cobb each focus their dramaturgical efforts on pedagogical and participatory modes of performance that invite audiences to engage directly with history and historiography. In the process, they each stage important conversations about the work of historical interpretation and access. Segal cultivates dramaturgical skills in student visitors to the Intrepid Museum (New York City) in order to teach historical research and interpretation through experiential learning. Flipping the traditional museum theatre format, in which audiences passively spectate, Segal's "Crossing the Line" program offers student participants the opportunity to create and perform original works devised from the museum's collections. Through an analysis of Bertolt Brecht's 1938 *Fear and Misery of the Third Reich (Furcht Und Elend Des Dritten Reiches)*, Todoruţ explicates Brecht's strategy of dramatizing historical injustice anti-dramatically or anti-spectacularly to render a more complex and polyvocal conception of the past. Importantly, Todoruţ notes, an anti-dramatic dramaturgy of oppression might also offer a greater sense of individual and collective agency to resist. Todoruţ then demonstrates how Brecht's anti-spectacular dramaturgical method can be implemented to similar effect through her work with a group of Chinese high school students confronting the pressure to conform and succeed. Drawing on her experiences co-creating a site-specific performance entitled "Beyond Land Acknowledgement" at Allerton Park & Retreat Center in Monticello, Illinois, Anderson Cobb provides readers with techniques for doing creative work in spaces with long histories of racial violence. Created with Latrelle Bright, Anderson Cobb's performance, art installation, and dialogue engaged the entangled histories of local Native tribes and settler colonial violence. In detailing her approach to welcoming BIPOC (Black, Indigenous, and People of Color) audiences to a site with a history of anti-Black racism,

Anderson Cobb advocates for dramaturgs to take up the mantle of community engagement, particularly in the context of reducing access barriers to performance, which take not only physical and financial forms but also cultural ones.

Laurie Arnold (Sinixt Band Colville Confederated Tribes) and Daphnie Sicre offer two distinct approaches to using dramaturgical skills to make minoritarian histories more widely and richly available. Together, these chapters highlight the benefits of interdisciplinary approaches and conversations between dramaturgy and history. Arnold draws on her expertise as a Native public historian to offer dramaturgs a guide for contextualizing, advocating for, and producing Native plays. Arnold provides dramaturgs tools for approaching Native work from a space of ethical responsibility and cultural competence through a discussion of *Off the Rails* by Randy Reinholz (Choctaw) and the publicly available archival materials that can be used to illuminate the histories of forced assimilation through boarding schools that are addressed in the play. Sicre outlines the stakes, considerations, challenges, and processes inherent to creating an AfroLatine theatrical archive. Sicre illustrates how dramaturgs can contribute to the documentation of vibrant histories of performance with an eye toward supporting future scholarship and public engagement. Collectively, the volume's authors demonstrate dramaturgy's capacity to generatively mobilize history and historical thinking in theatrical contexts, challenging limiting notions of the past as a monolithic and distant entity.

Note

1 In addition to the manuals cited here, see also, for example: Hartley, *The Shakespearean Dramaturg*; Irelan, Fletcher, and Dubiner, *The Process of Dramaturgy*.

Works Cited

Bly, Mark. "Bristling with Multiple Possibilities." *Dramaturgy in American Theater: A Source Book*, edited by Jonas, Susan, Geoffrey S. Proehl, and Michael Lupu, Harcourt Brace College Publishers, 1997, pp. 48–55.

Chemers, Michael Mark. *Ghost Light: An Introductory Handbook for Dramaturgy*. Southern Illinois University Press, 2010.

Hartley, Andrew James. *The Shakespearean Dramaturg: A Theoretical and Practical Guide*. Palgrave Macmillan, 2005.

Irelan, Scott R., Anne Fletcher, and Julie Felise Dubiner. *The Process of Dramaturgy: A Handbook*. Focus Publishing, 2010.

Jonas, Susan and Geoffrey S. Proehl, and Michael Lupu, eds. *Dramaturgy in American Theatre: A Source Book*. Harcourt Brace College Publishers, 1997.

Jonas, Susan. "Aiming the Canon at Now: Strategies for Adaptation." *Dramaturgy in American Theater: A Source Book*, edited by Jonas, Susan, Geoffrey S. Proehl, and Michael Lupu, Harcourt Brace College Publishers, 1997, pp. 244–65.

Mazer, Cary M. "Rebottling: Dramaturgs, Scholars, Old Plays, and Modern Directors." *Dramaturgy in American Theater: A Source Book,* edited by Jonas, Susan, Geoffrey S. Proehl, and Michael Lupu, Harcourt Brace College Publishers, 1997, pp. 292–307.

Proehl, Geoffrey S. "The Images Before Us: Metaphors for the Role of the Dramaturg in American Theatre." *Dramaturgy in American Theater: A Source Book,* edited by Jonas, Susan, Geoffrey S. Proehl, and Michael Lupu, Harcourt Brace College Publishers, 1997, pp. 124–36.

Romanska, Magda, ed. *Routledge Companion to Dramaturgy*. Routledge, 2015.

Scanlan, Robert. *Principles of Dramaturgy*. Routledge, 2020.

Part I

Production Dramaturgy

(Re)contextualizing Existing Plays

1 Experimenting with Conceptual Casting

Tennessee Williams's *The Glass Menagerie*

Khalid Y. Long

Tennessee Williams's *The Glass Menagerie* (1944) is one of the most revived plays in US American theatre. Set in St. Louis in 1937, the semi-autobiographical play centers on the Wingfield family: Tom; his sister, Laura; and their mother, Amanda. Throughout the play, audiences observe the members of the family struggle with the absence of the children's father, Amanda's overbearing care of her children, Laura's physical ailment and social anxiety, and Tom's desire to break free—literally and metaphorically—from the confines of the cramped family home. So, what does it mean when a semi-autobiographical play is produced through the lens of conceptual casting, and how might production dramaturgs support the implementation of such practices? What happens when productions "re-imagine the function of 'race' in plays" (Emeka 36)? What are the possibilities rendered when canonical works are staged through conceptual frameworks and casting?

For their 2021–2022 season, Rep Stage, a regional theatre in Howard County, Maryland, produced *The Glass Menagerie*. Under the guidance of producing artistic director Joseph Ritsch (also director of *The Glass Menagerie*), Rep Stage has been vocal about its commitment to anti-racist theatre practices, ranging from the diversity of shows produced to an inclusive casting policy. Additionally, Rep Stage routinely hires dramaturgs who specialize in the intersections of race, class, and gender, such as myself, to help with creative concepts that challenge the status quo embedded within canonical (read: white) dramas.

My standard dramaturgical practice is to connect with the director as early as possible to clarify their vision. Ritsch shared during our initial conversation that he wanted to embrace race-conscious casting. In this way, he hoped to explore "taking the image of family and expanding that image, especially from how it has historically been presented in this play" (qtd. in Wild). As such, my early conversations with Ritsch included us questioning the historical circumstances of the play. Admittedly, the concept—in terms of thematic and narrative possibilities—that we would ultimately move forward with did not come until the start of rehearsals. However, we were clear that the

DOI: 10.4324/9781032636337-3

casting of the actors and the resultant experimentation with the racial identities of the characters would eventually govern what would be possible. Grace Bauer, a white woman, was cast as Amanda quite early. Dylan Arredondo, a multi-racial actor (Japanese, white, and Mexican), was cast as Tom, and Brittany Davis, an African American woman, was cast as Laura. A white actor, Noah Israel, was cast as the Gentleman Caller.

I played no role in how the show was cast. However, upon being informed about the cast, I subsequently saw my duties as the production dramaturg divided into three areas: (1) to frame the type of inclusive casting that was being enacted; (2) to historicize inclusive theatre practices previously implemented in productions of *The Glass Menagerie*; and (3) to offer historical context, language, and possible scenarios that could shape the world of the play and the characters' reality as a result of the proposed casting.

Framing the Practice of Conceptual Casting

Whether one designates it as "cross-racial casting," "color-conscious casting," "blind casting," "conceptual casting," or "integrated casting," each of these practices indexes an attempt to be more diverse and inclusive. It is important to note that the implementation of such practices does not, on its face, guarantee the resulting production will be inclusive or anti-racist. Each of these practices has its detractors and proponents, but they all take on the difficult work of pushing the boundaries of the relationship between dramatic literature and stage performance to reflect the social, political, and cultural dynamics of the past and present. I began using the phrase "conceptual casting" in every setting—from meetings to rehearsal—to designate how "an actor is cast in a role to give a play greater resonance" (Clinton Davis Turner and Harry Newman qtd. in Catanese 12). Conceptual casting can help to reimagine canonical works, subsequently illuminating the power and viability of the theatre in the contemporary moment. My goal was to ensure that the cast and creative team became familiar with conceptual casting. In this way, we could emphasize the critical possibilities of differently attending to specific periods, historical events, and culturally specific subject matters through drama and performance—what some theatre practitioners recognize as a process of defamiliarization—thus encouraging the audience to think beyond what may have taken for granted as normal or standard. As it relates to anti-racist theatre, the process of defamiliarization can unsettle dominant ways of seeing a production and allow it to be seen through other lenses and perspectives. In that sense, the show belongs to no one particular person or group but invites everyone to participate in its (re)construction.

When it came to naming the precise casting practice we were utilizing, I recognized that specificity was essential to our ability to take responsibility for and be cognizant of the narrative being staged. The dramaturgical strategy being enacted needed to be understood within the larger context of nontraditional casting practices. If race was to be a central factor in how the show was cast, I wanted us to not only be specific in explicitly naming the type of casting practice that was endorsed but also in addressing how performers of color would be presented to audiences and how the cast's understanding of the play would change when distinctive attention was paid to the sociocultural and political themes evoked by their presence on stage. This dramaturgical strategy urges creative teams to critically discuss how a play's social, cultural, and political landscape will be altered when the race of select characters changes. This prompted me to research the history of actors of color performing in white-authored plays, including prior productions of *The Glass Menagerie*, aiming to locate productions that took the liberty of developing concepts that challenged conventional narratives.

Historicizing Inclusive Casting

The Glass Menagerie has proven to be a flexible play, meaning that the play has been adapted many times to fit a particular perspective or vision especially where "nontraditional casting" was concerned. Shortly after its 1945 Broadway premiere, theatre programs at historically Black colleges led the charge in producing what Philip Kolin recognizes as "a vital counter-tradition … to a dominant and potentially repetitious white theatre culture" ("Black and Multi-Racial Productions" 97). One production that stands out is Spelman College and Morehouse University's 1987 co-production directed by Thomas A. Brown. Spelman/Morehouse's co-production is a noteworthy example, for it was adapted to take place in the 1960s, thus highlighting the joy and tensions of the Civil Rights Movement. Brown wrote in his Director's Notes:

> I have set the play in the industrial westside of St. Louis during the early 1960s. At that time, all of America was poised for revolution. As a consequence, many "dreams" were being created while many 'myths' were being broken. […] In *The Glass Menagerie*, the Wingfield family is as much poised for revolution and the realization of dreams as was America.
>
> (qtd. in Kolin "Black and Multi-Racial Productions" 104)

Kolin contends that when casting classics with actors of color, "there are opportunities for enlarging the script, opening the plays up to racial and social messages that are not privileged in white productions" ("Tennessee Williams Scholars Conference Panel" 80). To be sure, the Spelman/Morehouse production served as a catalyst for me when impelled to consider the "racial and social messages" for Rep Stage's production.

Possible Scenarios: Shaping the World of the Play

During the first rehearsal, we discussed and implemented the "racial and social messages" that would arise due to how the show was cast. This proved urgent when one of the actors asked: "How will we justify this interracial family in the 1930s in St. Louis, Missouri?" Our director, Ritsch, deferred to me as we had previously chatted about the possible scenarios and background context to validate the casting choices. I responded, "Anti-miscegenation – that is, the prohibiting of interracial marriage – was the law of the land during that period, and so it will be a pragmatic choice for this production." This warranted a fuller backstory that didn't distort Williams's plot but instead filled in gray areas to complement the story. Fortunately, Williams's ambiguity about Mr. Wingfield's presence allowed us to develop the following scenario: Amanda married Mr. Wingfield while they still resided in the South. Mr. Wingfield was a man of color, and because of anti-miscegenation laws, they could not marry. They eventually married but got away with it because Mr. Wingfield was most likely white-passing. Thus, they fled the South and relocated to St. Louis to escape someone finding out about their illegal marriage. St. Louis was a major city where Blacks relocated during the Great Migration, giving credence to Mr. and Mrs. Wingfield's escape to the cosmopolitan city. We then deduced that Mr. Wingfield abandoned the family because someone found out about his white passing, thus threatening the family's safety. Through conceptual casting, we were able to disrupt accustomed or prescribed ideas of family—what Ritsch called expanding the image of family—by conceiving of a scenario that played within America's troubled history of race relations.

Using the history of anti-miscegenation laws, prompted by conceptual casting, proved valuable on several more fronts. It gave us the dramatic backstory needed to justify the interracial Wingfield family. Furthermore, it encouraged us to have critically honest conversations about race during rehearsals—further signaling the importance of having a dramaturg who specializes in race (among other aspects of identity) join rehearsals from the beginning. What we learned during the first week of rehearsal was that many of the performers did not necessarily think too deeply about race, historically or contemporarily. While this did not jeopardize our concept, the director and I discussed how imperative it was, especially for Amanda, to understand the seriousness and potential dangers of having biracial children in America during the 1930s. To remedy this, the director had me schedule one-on-one meetings with the cast to discuss how race was (becoming) central to the production. Understanding those cultural and political dimensions for Amanda would ultimately impact her relationship with her children, thus informing her acting choices. For instance, when Amanda learns that Laura has dropped out of Rubicam's Business College and has been wandering the city alone for weeks during the time of day when she is expected to be in school, the actress does not solely lean on Amanda's idiosyncrasies. She allows the scenario of Laura, a visibly

Black girl, wandering the streets of St. Louis to bear weight on how she reacts during that scene. Amanda's authoritarian parenting was reinscribed as an anxious mother concerned for her children because of the anti-Black sentiments of the time.

There were, however, some concerns that arose. Dylan Arredondo, who played Tom, said he would not portray Tom as a Black man. This was due in part to the actor's own multiracial identity. Thus, Arredondo anchored his portrayal in the looming presence of Tom's queer identity. Ritsch's approach to the text foregrounded the notion that Amanda had a wariness of Tom's queerness, consequently motivating her question of his whereabouts, especially during one of the more contentious moments of the play. Amanda challenges the notion that Tom has been attending the movies every night at the times he says he has, pointing out that movies aren't even screened in the early hours when he returns home. He must, she insists, be doing something shameful instead, and creating the movies excuse as a cover story. Because Ritsch wanted to underscore Tom's implicit queerness, I was charged with researching the queer spaces in St. Louis during the period. Ritsch knew of Dante's Inferno, the first gay bar in what would become St. Louis's gay district. My research yielded a more robust grasp of St. Louis's queer society, which gave rise to the notion that Tom had a community to which he belonged. For this production, Tom and Laura were quite affectionate toward each other, thus heightening the strained relationship the siblings have with their mother. For Laura, however, we focused on the notion that she was biracial: Black and white. In rehearsals, we focused on Laura's connection to her father, which Williams signifies through her attachment to his victrola. For example, I created a playlist of Black jazz artists of the early twentieth century for Davis to listen to, thus helping her develop her character's symbolic relationship with her absent father. Playing up Tom's queerness, as opposed to his mixed-raced identity, further augmented a kinship between brother and sister that went beyond bloodline. Intrinsically, their kinship was constructed through the (re)production of marginalized identities, which exposed audiences to two communities that have not always been centered in popular dramatic literature from this period.

Conceptual casting remains a complex and, in some cases, controversial practice within the performing arts industry. However, we must take seriously and implement dramaturgical methods informed by historical and cultural analysis that fittingly complicate our understanding of social positions, especially during periods that we are quite distanced from. In this way, dramaturgs working within conceptually cast productions might help surface what is latent in the play, prompting new explorations. This allows theatre artists to develop new creative strategies for staging canonical works that may allow actors of color to portray characters with a sense of authenticity and familiarity. Conceptual casting of canonical works can also defamiliarize well-known plays, thus mediating and presenting an innovative world for audiences to witness and celebrate.

Exercise

1 Choose a play commonly regarded as part of the US canon, featuring a traditionally predominantly white cast. For example, a play by Lillian Hellman, Eugene O'Neill, Tennessee Williams, Susan Glaspell, or Samuel Shephard.
2 Select one or more characters to cast in a different race (or other identity marker such as gender).
3 Read through the play and consider how changing the identity marker of a character(s) emphasizes or alters the cultural, political, and/or historical context of the play. In doing so, reflect on what gets underscored or heightened. Are there any problems that might need to be resolved through further historical research as a result of this casting?
4 Record and distill your findings. Then, develop a proposal for a conceptual framework that you might present to a director of the selected work.

Works Cited

Catanese, Brandi Wilkins. *The Problem of the Color[blind]: Racial Transgression and the Politics of Black Performance*. University of Michigan Press, 2011.

Emeka, Justin. "Playing with 'Race' in the New Millennium." *Casting a Movement: The Welcome Table Initiative*, edited by Claire Syler and Daniel Banks. Routledge, 2019, pp. 36–48.

Kolin, Philip C. "Black and Multi-Racial Productions of Tennessee William's The Glass Menagerie." *Journal of Dramatic Theory and Criticism*, vol. 9, no. 2, Spring 1995, pp. 97–128.

Kolin, Philip C. "Tennessee Williams Scholars Conference Panel: A Black Cat and Other Plays African American Productions of Williams's Drama." *The Tennessee Williams Annual*, no. 13, 2012, pp. 79–91.

Wild, Stephi. "Rep Stage Returns Live and in Person Next Month with *The Glass Menagerie*." *Broadway World*, 11 March 2022, broadwayworld.com/baltimore/article/Rep-Stage-Returns-Live-and-In-Person-Next-Month-With-THE-GLASS-MENAGERIE-20220311.

Williams, Tennessee. *The Glass Menagerie*. 1944. New Directions Publishing, 2011.

2 (Dis)Respecting Canonical Texts

Jennifer Popple

Since its 1953 premiere, Arthur Miller's play, *The Crucible*, has taken its place among the canonical works in American drama. *The Crucible* is lauded for its dual presentation of two unique moments in American history: the late seventeenth-century Salem witch trials and the Communist "witch hunts," led by Senator Joseph McCarthy, of the 1950s. Miller leveraged the historicized setting of the witch trials into an allegory for the contemporaneous "Red Scare," revealing their shared goals of repression and control.

The Crucible focuses its moral allegory on one man, John Proctor, who stands up against baseless accusations of witchcraft made against him and others by his former servant Abigail and her young female followers. In the end, John proudly goes to his death after righteously refusing to sign his name to a false confession that would free him from hanging. The text of the play leaves no doubt that John is the tragic hero, battling alone against the accusations, standing up for himself in a way that weaker people cannot or will not. He dies a virtuous hero, celebrated by the characters and the audience for choosing death over dishonor.

Today, directors and dramaturgs should hesitate when it comes to the ways Miller presents John; his devoted wife, Elizabeth; and Abigail, his former sexual partner. Miller's depiction of an honorable man who was led astray by a seductive young woman disguises the story of a man in a position of power who has taken advantage of his teenage employee. The fact that Proctor is held up as the virtuous hero while Abigail is presented as the villain has not aged well, especially when seen through the lens of the #MeToo movement. Any contemporary production of this work benefits from a critical engagement with the limitations in the original text through thoughtful dramaturgical work.

Exemplified through a production of *The Crucible* staged at Augustana College (Rock Island, IL) in 2019, this chapter details how dramaturgical work can illuminate and mitigate problems in canonical plays without changing one word of the text. This method takes up standard dramaturgical practices to crack the text open and make space for the marginalized figures in the piece. "(Dis)Respecting" canonical texts empowers dramaturgs

DOI: 10.4324/9781032636337-4

and directors to lean into the "both/and" of opportunities and limitations in the original script to elevate it to a relevant presentation for contemporary audiences.

When I chose *The Crucible* for the canonical work I would direct the following year, I knew the dramaturgical work would be challenging for my student dramaturg, Katie Kleve. As her advisor and director, I needed to guide her to actively question an inert script with original themes and messages that were limited and even toxic in our own time. My job was to help her do more than just revive a celebrated, canonical text; in this case, I needed to guide the student to use dramaturgical methodology to assist with the "transformation of a dramatic script into a *meaningful* living production" (Chemers 5, emphasis mine). This distinction would help us illuminate the problems in the original script more overtly, as the language, themes, and messages about women and their inherent guilt in *The Crucible* are too close to modern attitudes to risk not calling attention to them.

Step 1: Script Analysis and Research

The first step in a dramaturgical approach that (dis)respects the text is the same as the dramaturg's work on any play: conduct your script analysis, starting with what the author constructed. Kleve and I did repeated readings of the script, sharing our thoughts on the play's structure, the external and internal conflicts in the play, the major plot points, and the ultimate takeaway messages for the original audiences. We researched Salem, the original witch trials, and the real-life people who influenced Miller's presentations. When we found things that differed between real life and Miller's creations, we noted it. We couldn't know if every decision was purposeful and what may have been due to a lack of information, but we included the differences between historical record and artistic product in our notes.

This step is vital to the remainder of the artistic process, as it is the one that grounds the ensuing dramaturgical work in the building blocks of the original text. Regardless of whether or not one is analyzing canonical works that dramatize real events and historical figures, this step encourages historical research into the play's original context, encouraging the dramaturg to see the ways it connects to and/or pushes back against the religious, cultural, and political norms that the playwright was writing within. It requires curiosity, as opposed to judgment, and can open us to greater respect for the original text, despite whatever interpretation we know we want to bring to it.

We compared our research to Miller's play. Kleve placed those comparisons side by side, creating a document that had Miller's dramatic character on one side and the historical record of that same person on the other, as shown in Table 2.1.

Table 2.1 Sample comparison of historical figure and dramatic character by Katie Kleve

Abigail Williams (Arthur Miller)	*Abigail Williams (Historical Record)*
• 17 years old (16 or 17 at the time of sexual relationship with John)	• 11 or 12 years old at the time of witch trials
• Former servant to John and Elizabeth Proctor	• Not employed as servant
• Living with uncle, Reverend Parris; his daughter, Betty; and Tituba, a woman enslaved by Parris	• Living with uncle, Reverend Parris; his daughter, Betty; and Tituba and John Indian, a husband and wife enslaved by Parris
• Orphan since early childhood	• Unknown parental origins
• Described as beautiful and deceitful	• No known appearance or behaviors documented beyond the "fits" she had during the accusing phase
• Falsely accuses neighbors of witchcraft	• Falsely accused neighbors of witchcraft
• Escapes on a boat with her friend, Mercy	• Took part in the start of the trials but disappeared from public record halfway through the trials. No more is known about her after that.

After we constructed these comparisons, we looked at how the text worked with the advertent or inadvertent changes Miller had made. Although it was true that the fictional Abigail and the real-life Abigail started the witchcraft accusations, her role as a former "lover" of John Proctor's was a sharp departure from the historical record. It was this part of the story that caused the biggest problem for us, as John was an older, married man, and Abigail was his servant. Despite John's confession that he is guilty of infidelity, Miller presents Abigail as a malevolent force and the person to blame for their predicament.

Kleve and I discussed how we could present Miller's original story while also illuminating the power dynamics that are apparent from a modern lens. In this way, we engaged with what Wendy Schissel has termed the "an/Other reading": "one that reveals the assumptions of the text, the author, and the reader/critic who 'is part of the shared consciousness created by the play'" (461). In doing this an/Other analysis, Kleve highlighted the character descriptions, beats, and lines that Miller used to paint the characters as villain (Abigail), hero (John), and helpmate (Elizabeth). We looked for places in the play where opportunities could arise to animate more complicated readings of the characters.

I asked Kleve to conduct comparative studies of female characters in other Miller plays and to compile a literature review of feminist critiques of Miller's work. This critical research proved crucial to her ability to let go of a strict "guardianship" of the text and gave her the tools to examine *The Crucible* as an informed critic.

Step 2: Theory Work

The second step involved our application of feminist theory to the original text. When I teach theories in my dramaturgy class, I describe that work as comprising three options. The first one is to identify a theory that is already built into the play and find where the text shows it to us; Bertolt Brecht's work with Marxist theory serves as the simplest example of this type of theory work. The second option involves the application of a theory that might not be already built into the script but that the text responds to readily. For example, Brecht's *Mother Courage and Her Children*, which has Marxist theory built into it, suffers from a lack of intersectionality. A secondary Feminist theory layered on top of Marxist theory in *Mother Courage* illuminates the patriarchal norms in that play's setting. This is the option many directors choose when directing canonical texts. Shakespeare's plays, as an example, readily open up to a number of different theories, and many exciting productions have come out of the application of Psychoanalytic, Queer, Postcolonial, or Feminist theory to the classical play text.

The third option is the most delicate: the application of a theory that the text actively resists. This is the approach I took in my layering of Feminist theory over *The Crucible*. The play pushed back harder than any other I have ever applied a theory to, but I asked Kleve to note the places in which the text responded, where it offered spaces for opportunity, and where it resisted. The most exciting opportunity for us was a scene that is only referenced in the play, despite it providing the catalyst for the main plotline: the girls' Bacchanalian outing with Tituba in the woods.

We chose to stage the girls' escape into the woods as a pre-show movement piece, beginning with the girls conducting mechanical movements of "feminine" activities of the time (sewing, stirring a pot, caring for an infant), ending with a bell tolling signifying they could escape to the woods, where they were free: dancing, running, screaming, taking their hair down, and engaging in the voodoo rituals that Tituba offered as a place of escape from the rigidity of their Protestant society. When Betty Parris fell into her coma-like state, the girls gathered to carry her, tenderly settling her into her bed before retreating to the back of the stage. From there, they watched while the play opened on Reverend Parris praying at her bedside. This reframed the entire play around the girls' journey and the restrictive society in which they lived in a way the original text did not.

Whenever the text outright resisted, we had to pay special attention to our work. Without being able to change the words, we knew we would have to lean on movement, acting choices, and design to create spaces for the feminist message to seep through the problematic text. Kleve was essential in this step of the process, notating these moments of resistance from the text that I could take to my production team and problem-solve with. These problematic moments would still live in the final product but were complicated by our interventions.

Step 3: The Casebook

The creation of the casebook took all of this work and condensed it for our actors and production members. Actors were given a crash course in the #MeToo movement, and we worked in rehearsal to demonstrate the power dynamics of the time that these characters lived in while still encouraging actors to remain empathetic to their own characters.

Step 4: Engagement with the Audience

We extended our efforts to complicate the text in our audience engagement. Kleve's dramaturgical display in the lobby connected the characters to their historical counterparts, showing audiences who these people were and the real-life relationships they had or didn't have. One poster was dedicated to Tituba, showcasing her identity as an enslaved woman with information on voodoo in order to prepare audiences for a play that represents white Protestant fear of othered religious practices. The display also provided biographical information on Miller, including his admission that the dissolution of his first marriage (as a result of his affair with Marilyn Monroe) was part of the reason why he wrote the play ("Why I Wrote"). The other dramaturgical displays focused on the #MeToo movement, the Salem witch trials, McCarthyism, and the "Red Scare."

The production itself, grounded in the dramaturgical research described above, presented Abigail, Elizabeth, Tituba, and the other female characters as marginalized figures in a rigid, white supremacist, Christian patriarchy. Although their actions in the play are imperfect, our production aimed to empathetically elucidate why they may have felt they had no other chance to have power. It would not have been possible without the pre-production and production work of my student dramaturg described here.

The approach to (dis)respecting canonical texts can help inform other frequently villainized, thinly drawn, and/or misunderstood characters. My hope is that this case study encourages other artists to engage with canonical texts, facing them head-on in modern productions. Although there are a number of fascinating contemporary plays that critically engage with these canonical texts (by playwrights such as Paula Vogel, Sarah Ruhl, and Kimberly Belflower, among others), staging canonical texts can encourage dialogue with them and one another while we continue to look honestly at history. When we are assigned shows or asked to represent particular movements or times in theatre history that do not align with our own pedagogical goals and morals, we can approach canonical texts with a certain amount of irreverence and a challenging spirit to lift our productions into a more meaningful teachable space for us, our student actors, and our audiences.

Exercise

1 Choose a canonical play based on history. It can be a piece that drew from real people (William Shakespeare's *Julius Caesar* or Lillian Hellman's *The Children's Hour*) or a play that presents imaginary characters drawn from true events (Lope de Vega's *Fuente Ovejuna* and August Wilson's *Fences*).
2 Read the play and create a list of characters, using all identifying information given in the text.
3 Create a brief summary, summarizing the main plot and any subplots. Be brief (three to four sentences per scene), but hit the main points.
4 Research the real situation and/or characters the playwright dramatized. Use a variety of sources, including playwright interviews, newspaper articles, reviews, scholarly books and articles, and videos.
5 Create a side-by-side chart (using Table 2.1 as an example), comparing and contrasting the historical item and the dramatized creation (plot point or character).
6 Discuss the differences between the real history and its dramatic representation. Why might the playwright have decided to present history in this way? How does the author's revision of this history impact our understanding?
7 Then discuss if there is room to challenge or expand upon this dramatic interpretation in a production of the play. How and why might you go about doing this?

Works Cited

Chemers, Michael Mark. *Ghost Light: An Introductory Handbook for Dramaturgy*. 2nd ed. Southern Illinois University Press, 2023.

Miller, Arthur. *The Crucible*. 1952. Dramatists Play Service, 1982.

Miller, Arthur. "Why I Wrote *The Crucible*." *New Yorker*, 13 October 1996. https://www.newyorker.com/magazine/1996/10/21/why-i-wrote-the-crucible. Accessed 23 November 2022.

Schissel, Wendy. "Re(dis)covering the Witches in Arthur Miller's The Crucible: A Feminist Reading." Modern Drama, Volume 37, Number 3, Fall 1994, pp. 461–473.

3 Evoked, If Not Depicted

Dramaturgy and Local Histories

Charlie Peters

Plays depict and are themselves the products of specific histories. Many plays are experienced, however, in the context of very different histories than those which informed the plays' writing or those that they depict onstage. These histories are, of course, the (ongoing) histories of the places in which they are staged. Local histories are no less—and perhaps even more—significant to a production than the ones dramaturgs are more used to engaging. This chapter offers tools for exploring and engaging local histories relevant to a particular theatrical production, considering especially the play's themes and/or a production's goals. I explore this methodology using the case study of a production of Bertolt Brecht's *The Resistible Rise of Arturo Ui (Der aufhaltsame Aufstieg des Arturo Ui)* at Persephone Theatre in Saskatoon, Saskatchewan, Canada, in January 2018. In connection with this production, I co-developed an extra-theatrical audience engagement project exploring various forms of resistance employed by activists throughout the city's history and in the province of Saskatchewan more broadly which was inspired by the stated aims of the production.[1]

The Resistible Rise of Arturo Ui depicts the rise to power of a fictional Chicago gangster as he consolidates influence by intimidating businesses and misusing public funds. A satire of the rise of Adolf Hitler in 1930s Germany, the play features a title character based on Hitler and other characters that are lampoons of other figures significant in his pre-World War II government and military. The play allegorically depicts the escalation of fascism and includes fictionalized versions of actual events in German history. Brecht wrote the play in 1941 in Finland, having fled his native Germany for fear of Nazi persecution and while awaiting a visa, which would allow him to escape to the United States.

The play was included in Persephone's season as a response to the 2016 election of Donald Trump as President of the United States. This was articulated in public-facing materials as "these strange days when we can hardly believe what we see happening south of our border" ("The Resistible Rise"). Inspired by the timeliness of the production as much as the play's text, I worked with staff from Persephone Theatre to organize a lobby display in connection

DOI: 10.4324/9781032636337-5

with the production.[2] This display brought together protest signs that had been made and used locally in relation to a variety of social justice causes. To build the display, the theatre partnered with The Stand/Treaty Six Justice Collective, a nonprofit organization providing resources to grassroots groups and agencies working towards social, environmental, and economic justice. Without The Stand's deep community connections and local knowledge, the project would not have been possible. The lobby display was entitled *Answering the Call: A Visual Exhibition of Local Protest*. The protest signs were drawn largely from the personal archive of Saskatoon activist Don Kossick and were supplemented by commentaries written by members of The Stand to offer historical and social context. These commentaries were intersectional in framing and focused on three political movements in Saskatchewan—Labor and Farm Movements, Indigenous Rights Movements, and Peace and Global Solidarity Movements—with the work of women, students, elders, and IBPOC groups highlighted.

But why protest signs? And why local as opposed to the better-known protests of larger centers? Peter Hay argues that "theatre is a local phenomenon" (21). Many dramaturgs believe that the central question of their craft centers on why a particular play is being staged for a particular audience in a particular time and place (Chemers 108; Lang 79; Hay 13). Brecht's text works to convince its audience that the rise of fascism and authoritarianism is not inevitable, but rather resistible. The public framing of the play suggested that contemporary (and local) audiences also need to resist the re-emergence of these forces and be reassured that such resistance is possible. As Persephone put it, the play "sounds the alarm against the complacency of believing that the events of that era could never be repeated at another time in another place" ("The Resistible Rise"). Highlighting local resistance was meant to encourage audiences to consider tyranny to be resistible not only in the historical European context of the play's creation or the fictitious America in which the play is set but also in the local context in which it is experienced by audiences: in this place, at this time. Chemers argues that lobby displays provide an "opportunity for the dramaturg to cultivate the ideal mindset in the audience" (169). The write-up that accompanied the display emphasized both the province's "long history of people organizing to stand up for what they believe is right and to oppose what they believe is wrong" and the "alliance-building [that] has been an important part of creating change in Saskatchewan." The play's themes and the production's goals inspired the focus of the extra-theatrical engagement which worked to connect these themes and goals to the local history *evoked* by the play, rather than the (faux-)history *depicted* by the play or the historical circumstance which *informed* the play's creation. In keeping with Chemers's reminder that audiences experience lobby displays "before the show, at intermission, and after the show" (169), the display's lofty aim was not so much to support the audience's mindset going into the play (and therefore their reception of it), but rather to promote an activist mindset in its audience as they leave the performance (once the play has, ideally, inspired them).

My role with the theatre focused on audience engagement and not dramaturgy per se. This is due, in large part, to the role of dramaturg being understood in much of Western Canada as solely synonymous with new play development. While production dramaturgy work takes place here—including audience engagement work such as this project—it largely goes by other names. A major limitation of this framing of the work, however, was that my collaboration was almost exclusively with the theatre's marketing department. While the staff there were fabulous collaborators, marketing and audience engagement are not synonymous. The focus of marketing is getting bums in seats, while audience engagement is dedicated to deepening the experience of audience members, not necessarily increasing their numbers. The lobby display was envisioned as a stand-alone contribution to public discourse which did not require purchasing a ticket to the play. Although I was working with the marketing department, we thus worked to center audience engagement by ensuring the lobby was freely accessible to all, creating an opportunity for anyone who was interested to engage with this local history.

Engaging with the local is not without its risks. The curation of signs inspired the ire of a particular activist who felt that their cause had been unjustly excluded from the display. The display made no claims of being comprehensive, but this frustration points to the fraught and often political realities of working in community-engaged ways where interpersonal (or interorganizational or inter-movement) tensions can manifest. While we only received criticism for the content that we left out rather than what we chose to include, we understood that certain topics could have triggered backlash for their presence. No curation is neutral, and fear of backlash should not stop dramaturgs and their collaborators from making considered choices regarding which local histories to highlight.

One set of contemporary signs we foregrounded was from Idle No More, a grassroots movement

> [l]ed by women, and with a call for refounded nation-to-nation relations based on mutual respect [... which] rapidly grew into an inclusive, continent-wide network of urban and rural Indigenous working hand in hand with non-Indigenous allies to build a movement for Indigenous rights and the protection of land, water, and sky.
>
> (Idle No More)

We included several of the group's signs along with a narrative summary of their work. When investigating local history on colonized lands and in settler-colonial nation states (such as those on Turtle Island like Canada and the United States, as well as Aotearoa and Australia), settler colonialism and Indigeneity in relation to land are always already evoked. The call to action of Two-Spirit Cherokee scholar Qwo-Li Driskill is useful to consider: "While I don't think that scholars need to change the focus of their work, I *do* expect scholars to integrate Indigenous and decolonial theories into their critiques" (78). Highlighting the ongoing work of Idle No More as a major force of resistance in Saskatchewan and beyond was an attempt to draw attention to decolonial thought even in a work that does not explore decolonization. My colleagues at The Stand consulted with Indigenous scholars and activists with whom they had relationships to ensure that the portrayals of the movement in signs and writing were in keeping with how those movements wanted to present themselves, respecting what Garneau calls "irreconcilable spaces" where non-Indigenous participation is inappropriate (23). Working with respected, well-connected local partners allowed this to happen in a way that my relationships at the time and those of the theatre would not have allowed. We were not cold-calling an Elder with whom we had no relationship, but rather our collaborators were drawing on existing relationships built over years of work in solidarity.

Connecting the play's themes to local history was an attempt to acknowledge the importance of local resistance, without holding up a European man's writing as the final or best-developed word on resistance. Brecht is a European playwright firmly established in the so-called Western canon. Brecht's work is significant in the context of Western theatre history generally but is less—or, at best, differently—important in the context of Saskatchewan history, on the lands of the Nêhiyawak, Dene, Saulteaux, and Michif Nations, among many others. Brecht had likely never heard of this place and would not have known the names of the Nations who have cared for these lands since time immemorial. This is not necessarily to say his plays have no place in Saskatchewan. They will, however, carry additional and different layers of meaning in Saskatchewan than in Germany or even the United States (no less a colonial state but one more connected to Brecht as the place to which he was in the process of fleeing when he wrote the play).

Where a play is staged affects the meaning that can be made from it. Mohegan Tribal citizen Madeline Sayet, for example, refers to "The Shakespeare System" in the Americas. By this she means "not simply Shakespeare's written work, but the complex and oppressive role his work, legacy, and positionality hold in our contemporary society" ("Interrogating"). Working along racial and class lines, the plays are implicated in systems of oppression that extend into the dispossession of Indigenous lands. Algonquin and Irish theatre-maker Yvette Nolan refers to the "whitestream [... where] the standard is still Shakespeare, or the well-made play, or Aristotelian [...] form and content" (114). Plays from the European canon simply carry meaning differently on colonized lands than they do in Europe. Neither Sayet nor Nolan dismisses Shakespeare altogether, but both highlight how the elevation of European plays continues to serve as a tool of oppression. Brecht's plays are not part of the Canadian curriculum in the same way as Shakespeare, nor does Brecht carry the same prestige in this country. However, attention to Brecht as a canonical European playwright is an important consideration for local-history dramaturgy.

Persephone's 2018 production of *Arturo Ui* did not in itself focus on settler colonialism or decolonization—or, for that matter, anything local. The lobby display, however, strived to bridge the gap between the play and ongoing local histories. This project models just one of the ways in which local history can be explored in light of a play or production's themes and goals. Actively engaging with local history can be a creative dramaturgical challenge with the potential to add unexpected depths, relevance, and reach to a production.

Exercise

In order to consider where and how local history might inform dramaturgical work on a production, dramaturgs should ask the following questions early in their work on a project:

1. What are the themes of the play?
2. What are the goals of the production?
3. Where do you see these themes and goals being lived out, espoused, aspired to, or contested in the contemporary local context or local history?
4. Are there organizations or groups who have specialized knowledge of or interest in this history or whose values align with the goals of the production? How might you partner with them in ways that serve the production's goals *and* the goals of that organization or group? When in doubt, ask!
5. Who is Indigenous to the land on which this performance is taking place? https://native-land.ca/ is a great place to start.
6. What are the contemporary and historical politics of colonization in this place, and how do those intersect with the themes of the play or the goals of the production?
7. What is your/the theatre's situated relationship to the land and those Indigenous here? Is there much of a relationship? Be honest about this.
8. How might that relationship deepen, grow, or evolve for the better via this production while respecting irreconcilable spaces (see Garneau)?
9. In what ways might the knowledge gained, the relationships cultivated, and/or the truths explored in the questions above be best shared with an audience?
10. How might the always-already local nature of theatre be actively engaged within or (as with our lobby display) *around* the production?

Notes

1 I owe sincere thanks to Peter Garden who coordinated this work at The Stand/Treaty Six Justice Collective and provided invaluable connections to Saskatoon's activist community. I also owe thanks to Lisa Bayliss, Persephone Theatre's then Director

of Marketing who coordinated the Persephone Theatre side of the project. These two did as much as – or more than – I did to make this lobby display happen. Thanks to Stephen Rutherford, who did graphics and signage for the project and provided information for this chapter, and to Sum Theatre, a community-engaged independent theatre in Saskatoon, with which I was working as Artistic Associate when I was seconded to Persephone Theatre.

2 This was part of an audience-engagement-focused secondment (temporary job transfer) from Sum Theatre where I was working as an Artistic Associate to Persephone Theatre. Since Sum Theatre focuses on community-engaged work, part of the arrangement was that I would coordinate audience-engagement projects for shows in Persephone's season.

Works Cited

Chemers, Michael Mark. *Ghost Light: An Introductory Handbook for Dramaturgy*. Southern Illinois University Press, 2010.

Driskill, Qwo-Li. "Doubleweaving Two-Spirit Critiques: Building Alliances between Native and Queer Studies." *GLQ: A Journal of Lesbian and Gay Studies*, vol. 16, no. 1–2, 2010, pp. 69–92.

Garneau, David. "Imaginary Spaces of Conciliation and Reconciliation: Art, Curation, and Healing." *Arts of Engagement: Taking Aesthetic Action in and Beyond the Truth and Reconciliation Commission*, edited by Dylan Robinson and Keavy Martin. Wilfrid Laurier University Press, 2016, pp. 21–41.

Hay, Peter. "American Dramaturgy: A Critical Re-Appraisal." *Performing Arts Journal*, vol. 7, no. 3, January 1983, pp. 7–24.

Idle No More. "AN INDIGENOUS-LED SOCIAL MOVEMENT." *IdleNoMore.ca*, https://idlenomore.ca/about-the-movement/.

Lang, Theresa. *Essential Dramaturgy: The Mindset and Skillset*. Routledge, 2017.

Nolan, Yvette. *Medicine Shows: Indigenous Performance Culture*. Playwrights Canada Press, 2015.

Sayet, Madeline. "Interrogating the Shakespeare System." *HowlRound Theatre Commons*, 31 August 2020, https://howlround.com/interrogating-shakespeare-system.

"The Resistible Rise of Arturo Ui." *Persephone Theatre*.

4 Punk Nuns and Early Modern Vacationlands

Dramaturgical Approaches to Staging Sor Juana in the Twenty-First Century

Alison Hyde Pascale

When I signed on as dramaturg for an English language production of *Los Empeños de Una Casa* by Sor Juana Inés de la Cruz, I was immediately enticed by director James Ijames's vision of a contemporized production. Interested in diversifying the voices presented in the "classics" slot beyond Shakespeare or Greek tragedy, the Villanova Theatre season selection team for 2022–2023 chose Sor Juana's not-quite comedy of manners, originally written in 1683 by the Mexican nun for a festival in the capital of New Spain. Sor Juana herself and her personal history became an immediate touchstone for me, and for many others on the production. The underpinning of my dramaturgical interventions was Sor Juana's unique social position as a young, brilliant woman philosopher, proto-women's rights activist, and early queer icon (Stavans 20). I situated her as an important figure for multiple social movements in Latin America early in the production process, highlighting the relevance of her and her work in the contemporary world. As I said to the production team: she was a punk nun, and her work should be treated as such.

There is a significant cultural history of imaginative contemporary (re)stagings of Early Modern drama. The role of the Shakespearean director, for example, has been one of a re-inventor and re-imaginer for decades, finding places where the Bard's works intersect with and illuminate contemporary life. In his guide on Shakespearean dramaturgy, Andrew James Hartley advocates that dramaturgs should consider Shakespeare's work "not as the trappings of cultural nostalgia and elitism, but as cultural products that communicate – and therefore entertain, move, provoke, instruct, and so forth – right NOW and for whomever comes to watch them on stage" (7). Sor Juana's dramatic work is no less full of relevant opportunities to entertain, move, or provoke than Shakespeare, and presenting her voice on the contemporary stage opened an opportunity to not only begin ameliorating the lack of female voices presented on stage from the "classical" period, but also open crucial discussions about ethnocentrism, the Eurocentric canon, colonialism,

DOI: 10.4324/9781032636337-6

and institutionalized racism and sexism, all of which informed my dramaturgical interventions while working on this piece.

Because of these larger prejudices and cultural norms in the United States, audiences are less likely to anticipate or demand the staging of Early Modern work by writers other than Shakespeare. Aside from brief mention in theatre history textbooks, Sor Juana is largely unknown and un-produced outside of the Spanish-speaking world. These same norms preclude audiences from contemplating the possibility of contemporary reimaginings of Sor Juana's work. Because of his position as the paragon of the singular white male genius and the absolute ubiquity of his work on the English language stage, Shakespeare's plays are oft imagined as universal and malleable, able to be set in outer space or corporate offices or the American election circuit. However, I argue that audiences benefit from productions of lesser-known Early Modern work that focus on the "right NOW" and present diverse historical voices as possessing their own urgency and relevance to the contemporary moment.

As a dramaturg for the Villanova Theatre 2022 production of *House of Desires*, translated by Catherine Boyle, I focused on using historical context to feed the immediacy of the production. Below, I have divided my approach into three distinct interventions, including supporting and augmenting a director's vision, orienting the production team to a dialogic relationship with the play text, and providing a robust contemporary context for the production that dislodges notions of the play as antiquated.

Figure 4.1 Don Pedro (Sheldon Shaw, C) courts Dona Leonor (Emma Drennan, R) in front of his sister Dona Ana (Teya Juarez, L). Photo by Paola Nogueras.

Interventions

1 **Identify areas for edits, additions, and cuts in line with the director's vision**

Setting the text—cutting together editions of a play and otherwise editing to produce a playable script for a particular production—is a task that frequently falls to the dramaturg for an Early Modern work. Our distinct directorial vision was provided by James Ijames, best known as the Pulitzer Prize-winning playwright behind *Fat Ham*, a modern adaptation of *Hamlet* that re-envisions the titular character as a Black queer youth in the US South, which premiered on Broadway in 2023. As exemplified by *Fat Ham*, Ijames has shown a unique interest in reimagining historical texts and circumstances across his career as a playwright and director. His world for Boyle's *House of Desires* was similarly modernized, inspired by the contemporary Mexican vacation destinations of Cancún and Acapulco. Ijames riffed on reality TV programs with resonant themes of love and power, like *The Real Housewives* and *Too Hot to Handle*, which served as my inspiration in writing the pre-show speech.[1]

Along these lines, I identified additional areas that could benefit from contemporizing, drawing on pop culture references and the fandom surrounding Sor Juana in Latin America. *Los Empeños de Una Casa* features a song about the trials of love, a common element of comedy at the time. However, most modern translations rendered the humor very conservatively, leaving this large section of the script difficult to stage in an engaging manner. While collating and comparing translations of the song, I created and shared my own ultra-modern translation, which was ultimately utilized by Ijames and sound designer Jordan McCree. My Gen Z-friendly translation, which featured such trials of the heart as "catching feelings" —the equivalent of which was present in the original text—resonated with university student audiences, many of whom cited the song as their favorite part of the performance. As illustrated by the pre-show speech, Ijames utilized Sor Juana's original text to create a world, which echoed—and in its most salient moments held a mirror to—our own. As production dramaturg, I sought every opportunity to further the production's goal of creating a relatable world through suggestions and interventions like my translation of the song.

2 **Reorient actors away from textual supremacy toward a dialogic relationship with the text**

One of my main concerns as a dramaturg was encouraging the production team to see themselves as in dialogue with, rather than adherents to, the play text. Because we were presenting an English-language production of a work originally written in Spanish, our cast and creative team faced an additional layer of complication: we were working at an acknowledged remove from the original language. Moreover, our actors had the tendency to treat the script with the perceived reverential immutability of a Shakespearean text, which is itself a misconception about the absolute authority and singularity of English-language Early Modern play texts. As scholar of Early Modern Spanish theatre Catherine Larson points out, "an insistence upon faithfulness to the source fails to take into account the play in its newly embodied form and the modern audiences who interact with it" (22). Our actors had the sense that they must be "faithful" to the text. However, this was a misguided urge, as the text itself was already removed from its original meanings and context. Of course, this is true even for texts like Shakespeare's plays which are often viewed as singular and authentic, but actually interpolate multiple sources and exist in multiple versions.

One method I employed to demonstrate that both transliteration and reading across time inherently and generatively transform a text was to introduce the cast to multiple translations when appropriate. This aided in both clarifying moments where actors were unclear about the meaning of the script and illuminating the choices translators make in terms of elements like rhyme, rhythm, brevity, and clarity. My hope in introducing multiple translations during the rehearsal process was to move actors away from a dogmatic adherence to the text and toward an investment in clarifying the story our production told. This shift was supported in great deal by the dramaturgical research I presented to the production team about the ongoing relevance of Sor Juana as a rebel in her time and a countercultural figure of resistance. This approach toward the text as a living document supported Ijames's efforts to contemporize the world and situate the text within a dialogue between our cast, our creative team, multiple translators and editors across space and time, and Sor Juana herself. Included below is an exercise I completed with our cast during our first rehearsal, aimed at introducing the wide variance in tone and meaning different translations provide.

3 **Provide a robust contemporary context for the production that dislodges notions of the play as antiquated**

Uninitiated audiences are likely to expect a production of an Early Modern work to reproduce an imagined past. This sense may be intensified in the case of Sor Juana, whose identity as a Mexican woman (presumed to be "specific" where white cis-male perspectives are presumed to have an unacknowledged ability to express universal truths) might relegate stagings of her work to an archaic, turreted past. This marginalization of Sor Juana into a niche position in history results in her work not being regarded with the same timelessness and malleability which has been oft granted to European male writers, like Shakespeare. As the dramaturg, I utilized every opportunity to introduce the contemporary world of our play before the curtain went up, with the hope of orienting audiences toward relevant context, like Sor Juana's position in contemporary Mexican culture (i.e., her "punk-ness"), which aligned Sor Juana's world with the present moment.

I sought to manage audiences' expectations about the historical or "stuffy" nature of an Early Modern play written by a nun. In materials made available to audiences, I kept a focus on both the universal and contemporary relevance of Sor Juana's work. To highlight universal relevance, such as the trials of love, I included a lobby display asking audiences to anonymously contribute "the craziest thing you've ever done for love" citing the "hiding, lying, stealing, and cheating, all in the name of love" undertaken by the characters in the play. Responses were included on a corkboard in the lobby for the run of the production.

To highlight Sor Juana's specific contemporary relevance, I focused my audience-facing dramaturgical note on her Mexican countercultural status and her unique position as a historical figure regularly regarded as ahead of her time (Stavans 20). I emphasized Sor Juana's early life as a genius in her own right, her incredible literary output, her resistance against authority in her time, and her afterlife as a countercultural icon and proto-feminist. This primer introducing the history of the play as inherently transgressive readied audiences for a contemporized version of the play, which eschewed traditional period-appropriate staging. As there have been fewer than five English-language productions of *Los Empeños de Una Casa*, it was unlikely our audiences had interacted with Sor Juana's work before. Although this unfamiliarity required us to navigate audiences' expectations for the production, it also gave us an opportunity to present Sor Juana's work not as a relic but as a living document created in a countercultural context primed for reinterpretation.

There is extraordinary benefit to producing works encountered more commonly in the archive or the textbook than on the stage. It gives audiences and production teams the opportunity to engage with rich, storied, and challenging material, which often possesses as much if not more contemporary relevance than plays more commonly encountered in the "classics" season selection spot. Dramaturgs serve an important role in not only providing contextual information but also highlighting relevance to the here and now, effectively reanimating, rather than uncovering, plays from the archive.

Exercise

Sixty-Second Scenes: Rendition Mayhem

This exercise illuminates the significant effect translation and/or modernization have on the meaning and style of plays from the Early Modern period.

It highlights the difficult work of translation and modernization for comedic works and draws attention to the translators, adapters, and other mediators who play a key role in our contemporary understanding of Early Modern texts.

Choose a Scene

Choose a short excerpt with two to three characters spanning five to six lines. The most effective scenes will have humor and a button in the last line that lends a sense of completeness.

1 **Identify Translations and/or Editions**
   Rather than use the translation/edition being produced, choose two other translations or editions, if available. These should vary in tone—ideally, you will be able to contrast rhyming versus blank verse, contemporary prose versus Early Modern language, etc. The right scene choice will make these differences apparent. Lastly, run the scene from the original script through an online translation service or artificial intelligence (AI) text generator, prompting it to contemporize the language—the results will likely be independently humorous. You should include this translation along with the others without immediately disclosing its source.

2 **Stage Your Scenes**
   Break your production team into groups of two or three, depending on the number of characters in your scene. Ideally, no one will be assigned to their actual role. Using props and costume pieces, give the groups sixty seconds to stage their scenes. Then, have each group perform. Between performances, ask the whole group what the translator or adapter of that scene valued—clarity or prosody, brevity or richness, etc. Finally, reveal the different translators, including information on their stated intentions or other context for the translation if available. Point out the distinct difference between the scenes which were translated or edited, versus the one run through an online generator.

Note

1 Transcript of the pre-show speech: "Previously on House of Desires: Dona Ana and her assistant Celia have been vacationing at Ana's brother, Don Pedro's house: Casa de Pedro! Dona Ana has left her longtime boyfriend Don Juan to pursue Don Carlos, her hot new neighbor. Meanwhile, Carlos is in love with Dona Leonor, the most beautiful woman in the region. Pedro is also trying to woo Leonor! However, Leonor has planned to run away and elope with Carlos. Leonor's mother Dona Rodrigo and her right-hand man Hernando are completely unaware of this plan! And Carlos' assistant Castaño is still on the hunt! For a snack!"

Works Cited

De la Cruz, Sor Juana Inés. *House of Desires*. Translated by Catherine Boyle. Oberon Classics, 2004.

Hartley, Andrew James. *The Shakespearean Dramaturg: A Theoretical and Practical Guide*. Palgrave Macmillan, 2005.

Larson, Catherine. "Translating and Adapting the Classics: Staging La dama boba in English." *Bulletin of the Comediantes*, vol. 67 no. 1, 2015, pp. 19–36. Project MUSE, doi: 10.1353/boc.2015.0014.

Stavans, Ilan. *Sor Juana: Or, the Persistence of Pop*. University of Arizona Press, 2018.

5 *[Re]Fashion*ing Mowatt's Comedy of Manners through Adapturgy

Janna Segal

In *Adapturgy: The Dramaturg's Art and Theatrical Adaptation*, Jane Barnette introduces the term "adapturgy" to describe the dramaturgical work specific to adapting a source for stage production. Barnette defines "adapturgy" as "the dramaturgical intervention that connects the audiences to the choices that adapter and director have made for the production in question" (80). Published in 2017, Barnette's model for stage adaptation predates the COVID-19 suspension of in-person theatre; therefore, it does not address the adapturgy required of theatrical adaptations designed for performance through the virtual modalities many used in 2020–2021. Furthermore, because Barnette focuses on stage adaptations of nontheatrical texts familiar to audiences from "the American literary canon: novels written by white patriarchs, the plots of which are typically considered to be 'required reading' for secondary education" (21), she does not address the adapturgy required of stage adaptations of plays or lesser-known works. However, as Barnette notes, her strategies "apply to all theatrical adaptations" (2), and adapturgy is "an emerging field" whose parameters should be expanded (4).

I share the adapturgy undertaken by me and my collaborators to render Anna Cora Mowatt's 1845 play *Fashion* into a 2021 online production for the University of Louisville's Department of Theatre Arts. Mowatt's satire of the US American nouveau riche's Francophilia follows Mr. and Mrs. Tiffany's efforts to socially ascend through the marriage of their daughter, Seraphina. While Mrs. Tiffany aims to wed Seraphina to Count Jolimaitre, a cook masquerading as a French aristocrat, the financially compromised Mr. Tiffany is blackmailed into promising his daughter's hand to his clerk, Snobson. The knot of intrigues is unraveled by Adam Trueman, a rich, unpretentious farmer, and Gertrude, Seraphina's level-headed governess and Trueman's granddaughter. The reworked script was directed by Dr. J. Ariadne Calvano, dramaturged by me, and adapted by Calvano and me with input from our cast and assistant director, Blair Potter. We titled it *[Re]Fashion* to pronounce that it was a revision of Mowatt's mid-nineteenth-century play and of a historical narrative. Due to the pandemic, our rendition of Mowatt's comedy of manners was developed, rehearsed, and delivered via Zoom, with live-streamed

DOI: 10.4324/9781032636337-7

performances available on the Department's *YouTube* page from January 28–31, 2021. The adapturgical methods utilized to reproduce this historic comedy online and to make the source text's historical context accessible to a remote, contemporary audience include pursuit of a guiding adapturgical question; use of social media to conjure the lesser-known author and play's history; addition of a narrator whose interjections critique the source's white supremacist underpinnings; and inclusive casting designed to amplify historically marginalized voices, including those silenced by Mowatt's text. While these techniques were used for an online production of an oft-neglected play from American theatre's archives, they can be used for in-person productions of plays rendered less visible in the historical record.

Adapting Adapturgy's Ur-Question

Barnette proposes that the dramaturgs' "ur question" (18) "Why this play now?"—championed by Michael Mark Chemers (Chemers 108)—be altered by the adaptation dramaturg to "*why this source as theatre now*?" (Barnette 139). Barnette's question is suited for a stage rendering of a novel that must be transformed to function "as theatre" within an in-person theatrical space. As co-adapter and dramaturg of a theatrical revision for an online performance of a work written for the stage, I was guided by an alteration of Barnette's version of the dramaturgs' "ur-question": "Why this *dramatic* source as *online* theatre now?" My revision of the "ur-question" concentrates on adapting a work intended for stage production to a virtual platform.

Our two-part answer to this ur-question guided our work. We adapted Mowatt's *Fashion* partly to spotlight a play penned by a female playwright and actress who, despite calls for gender inclusivity, remains on the margins of the US American theatre canon. Sally Burke insists in *American Feminist Playwrights* that "by creating the most successful native comedy to appear on the American stage in the nineteenth-century—made-in-America social satire—Mowatt established for herself an important chapter in theatrical history" and "became a major contributor to feminist drama in America" (26). Yet, Mowatt and her "native comedy" do not appear in the anthologies typically used in dramatic literature courses, such as the *Norton Anthology of Drama.* She has fared slightly better in oft-taught theatre history textbooks like Brockett and Hildy's *History of Theatre*, where she receives one paragraph (319). Producing an adaptation of Mowatt's *Fashion* would therefore write into the received narrative of American theatre a fact that has been largely relegated to a footnote in the historical record: a female-identifying theatre artist helped shape American comedy of manners.

In addition to rewriting Mowatt into the historical record, we were motivated by the relevance of the play's critique of self-fashioning, which an online production could highlight. Mowatt's satire of mid-nineteenth-century America's fetishization of French fashions and obsession with self-representation resonated with twenty-first-century America's fixation on self-marketing and social media. Just as the Tiffanys and Seraphina's suitors adopt public personas, social media allows Americans to broadcast alternative selves. Because of the pandemic-necessitated shift to an online modality, we knew we would be reshaping Mowatt's comedy for performance by actors in remote locations and for delivery to audiences via screens. We felt the Zoom box frame around each character would emphasize the parallel between the self-fashioning satirized in Mowatt's script and that which we routinely practice through our online personas. The virtual medium enhanced the message, rendering *[Re] Fashion* more relevant to our social media-savvy university audience than could have been achieved through in-person theatre.

Social Mediating Mowatt

The paratheatrical materials I developed further capitalized on the online medium to deliver *[Re]Fashion*'s message. Barnette stresses, "the work of adapturgy includes the task of helping assure that spectators have some grounding in the source" (48). Through this "grounding," the dramaturg shares with audiences what Barnette describes as the conjuring "spirit" of adaptation, an uncanny "experience of communing with the source and/or its author" (49). Such communion is harder to create with a less familiar work like *Fashion*. To introduce audiences to Mowatt and *Fashion*, I conjured the author's spirit and the play's history using familiar, online self-marketing tools available via social media. Unable to ground virtual audiences in the source via a paper program or lobby display, I launched Facebook and Instagram pages for Mowatt that were followed and circulated by the production team. In the run-up to the production, I posted daily as the deceased author. These posts featured altered text from Mowatt's *Autobiography of an Actress* (1853), as well as archival images and production materials. For instance, as Mowatt, I wrote:

> Yesterday evening I sat in on a rehearsal for the UofL Theatre Arts production of *[Re]Fashion*. I do hope you will be able to virtually attend the live-streamed production of this adaptation of *Fashion*, which, when it premiered at the Park Theatre in 1845, marked my debut as a professional playwright. It gave me an odd sensation to hear my own language uttered in all varieties of tones, and often conveying a meaning of which I did not suppose it to be susceptible.

Borrowing Mowatt's recollection in her *Autobiography* of her "odd" experience watching the first rehearsal of *Fashion* (206), the post was accompanied by an archival image of Mowatt and our production poster, which appropriated that of the 1850 London production of *Fashion*. This social media campaign was a practical substitute for a program and lobby display that illustrated the relationship between Mowatt's play's critique of self-fashioning and the ways in which we now routinely perform personas on screens.

Fashioning a Narrator

The social media campaign launched alongside the production also supported our desire to see Mowatt written more forcefully into the historical record for having "Americanized the comedy of manners" (Burke 26). Uplifting Mowatt's place in history should not forestall critique of her work, especially given its reiteration of racist tropes. Mowatt's script launches with expositional dialogue between Millinette, a French lady's maid, and Zeke, who is described in Mowatt's character list as a "colored Servant" (NP) and who was performed at *Fashion*'s 1845 premiere by George Skerrett, a white, comic actor (Barnes 135; Butler 121; Mowatt, *Autobiography* 208). Consistent with the theatrical conventions of mid-nineteenth-century American theatre, this blackface role perpetuates racist stereotypes that we did not want to reanimate. We also did not want to ignore this aspect of Mowatt's script, lest we disregard the white supremacy that has underwritten American theatre since the country's founding. Calvano and I were exploring how to recognize without reinscribing *Fashion*'s racism when, in June 2020, the "We See You" collective called upon White American Theatre to reckon with the "white fragility and supremacy" upon which American theatre was built and continues to operate ("Statement"). Acknowledging *Fashion*'s role in consolidating American commercial theatre as a white industry was an answer to the We See You collective's call.

To acknowledge without recirculating *Fashion*'s racist stereotypes, we removed Zeke and added an omnipresent narrator named Professor Reddi Turner who bridged the off- and on-screen worlds. Our interlocutor was modeled after nineteenth-century African American scholar Anna Julia Cooper (1858–1964), whose *A Voice from the South* (1892) was published roughly twenty years after Mowatt's death. Played by African American performer Brandi LaShay and present throughout with book and pen in hand, Professor Reddi Turner was a constant reminder to the audience of (1) the absence of authentic Black voices in Mowatt's script and in early American commercial theatre and (2) the adaptation's efforts to write a more inclusive narrative. We replaced *Fashion*'s opening scene between Millenette and Zeke with a direct address from Professor Turner. This prologue, which included excerpts from Cooper's *A Voice from the South*, provided background information on Mowatt, the revision's setting, and the characters, including the excised role of Zeke. Holding a book and pen, Professor Turner pronounced the intention behind Zeke's removal:

> Zeke's function in Mowatt's play is primarily to demean and insult all those of African descent. It has been 175 years since the play was first

> produced in America; yet, the stereotypes circulated by such blackface roles as this still linger. Rather than erase these facts, we want to recognize these truths; recognize that re-fashion is the latest fashion. Rework the script to revoke the racist role. Remind us of the past without pretending that it never existed. (2)

Zeke was thus removed without neglecting the source's participation in circulating white supremacist ideologies. Professor Turner's interjections and omnipresence with writing tools kept upfront the adaptation's efforts to reshape received historical narratives by asking, in Professor Turner's words, "How is history refashioned, and by whom?" (2).

Recasting *Fashion*

Our approach to casting *[Re]Fashion* was another way we reckoned with the structural racism in Mowatt's play and in white American theatre. Barnette writes, "the question of representation, especially with regard to casting, is one of the ways that theatrical adaptation can reify or challenge societal norms and representations of history" (124). Casting was key to our attempts to pressure social prescriptions and historical narratives that were circulated by the comedy when it was first produced and that are in circulation today. *Fashion* was written for and first performed by an all-white cast whose roles aligned with their designated genders. For example, Mr. Tiffany was played by Mr. Barry, whose offstage wife, Mrs. Barry, played Mrs. Tiffany (Barnes 135; Butler 121; Mowatt, *Autobiography* 208). We used an inclusive casting approach aligned with the "identity-conscious casting" advocated by Lavina Jadhwani, which encourages actors' self-identities to inform the production. We cast nonbinary, trans, and BIPOC (Black, Indigenous, and People of Color) actors in parts of their choosing and shaped the script in accordance with their input on how their self-identity informed their character. To further address white American theatre's history of exclusionary practices for spectators, Professor Turner's prologue included a casting reveal. Professor Turner said to the remote audience:

> The historical record tells us that the original cast of Mowatt's *Fashion* was a group of all-white, cis-gender, able-bodied actors who recall the kind of casting we typically see in commercial theatre and film today. If this production were cast today as it would have been when the play premiered in 1845, and if we had an unlimited budget, this is what the cast would like,

at which point the performers' *"cameras turn[ed] on to reveal images of famous, white, cis-gender film actors"* (2). Professor Turner then said, "Rather than repeat this traditional mode of representing history and fiction, we took this approach," upon which our performers were "*revealed on the screen*" (2). Professor Turner concluded, "In this revision of an often-neglected play from the American past, our cast will reflect our present" (2). Pronouncing the inclusive casting upfront interrogated Mowatt's play's representational strategies and American media's exclusionary history. It also encouraged white, cisgender-heterosexual viewers to consider their socially conditioned acceptance of white, heteronormative stage and screen reflections of reality that do not mirror America's diversity.

Our refashioning of Mowatt's comedy of manners adapted a neglected, problematic, landmark, and relevant comedy for an online audience. Our adapturgical methods connected remote spectators to Mowatt's play without erasing the historical legacies of racism encoded in the source. While designed for an online production, these techniques could be employed for in-person endeavors to refashion less-familiar plays from the archives while attending to the issues raised by and through those historic texts.

Exercise

To develop your dramaturgical intervention, look at historical texts adjacent and contrary to the source play. Choose one of those contemporaneous texts that counters any view(s) in the source that you seek to problematize. Conjuring the spirit of that contemporaneous text's author, write a review of the source play. As you write your adaptation, dramaturgically utilize the channeled counter-voice's critique of the source. Maybe the conjured reviewer becomes your script's interlocutor. Perhaps their concerns guide the revision's plot, dialogue, or casting. The conjured review could even be recrafted into paratheatrical materials that frame your adaptation for the audience.

Works Cited

Barnes, Eric Wollencott. *The Lady of Fashion: The Life and the Theatre of Anna Cora Mowatt*. Scribner's, 1954.

Barnette, Jane. *Adapturgy: The Dramaturg's Art and Theatrical Adaptation*. Southern Illinois University Press, 2017.

Brockett, Oscar G., and Franklin J. Hildy. *History of the Theatre*. 10th ed. Pearson, 2008.

Burke, Sally. *American Feminist Playwrights: A Critical History*. Twayne, 1996.

Butler, Mildred Allen. *Actress in Spite of Herself: The Life of Anna Cora Mowatt*. Funk and Wagnalls, 1966.

Calvano, J. Ariadne, Janna Segal, et al. *[Re]Fashion*. Unpublished, 2020.

Chemers, Michael Mark. *Ghost Light: An Introductory Handbook for Dramaturgy*. Southern Illinois University Press, 2010.

Jadhwani, Lavina, and Victor Vazquez. "Identity-Conscious Casting: Moving Beyond Color Blind and Color-Conscious Casting." *Howlround*, 2 February 2021, https:/howlround.com/identity-conscious-casting.

Mowatt, Anna Cora. *Autobiography of an Actress; or, Eight Years on the Stage*. 1853. Hardpress Publishing, 2019.

Mowatt, Anna Cora. *Fashion; or, Life in New York*. W. Newberry, 1850. *InternetArchive*, 17 July 2021, https:/archive.org/details/fashionorlifeinn00ritc/page/n7/mode/2up.

Segal, Janna. "Yesterday Evening I Sat in on a Rehearsal for the UofL Production of [Re]Fashion." *Facebook*, 26 January 2021, https:/www.facebook.com/annacora.mowatt.

We See You. "Statement." *WeSeeYouWAT*, 8 Jun. 2020, www.weseeyouwat.com/statement.

6 History Looking Back

Dramaturging the Gaze

Yiwen Wu

On October 17, 1834, when the Carnes brothers' stock-in-trade cargo ship sailed into New York Harbor full of tea and fancy Chinese goods, a special passenger received mention in the *New-York Daily Advertiser*:

> The ship Washington, Capt. Obear, has brought out a beautiful Chinese Lady, called *Julia Foochee ching-chang king*, daughter of *Hong wang-tzangtzee king*. As she will see all who are disposed to pay twenty-five cents. She will no doubt have many admirers.
>
> (qtd. in Haddad 9)

Her lengthy name in the advertisement was meant to imitate the cadence of Cantonese, signifying nothing more than its foreignness—reduced to noise.

Two weeks later, she adopted a newer, simpler name, "Afong Moy," likely a generic nickname for women in Cantonese.[1] Over the next seventeen years, the name Afong Moy appeared in advertisements and museum records throughout the Mid-Atlantic, New England, the South, the Midwest, and even in Havana, Cuba.[2] Known as "The Chinese Lady," she was first put on display by merchant brothers Francis and Nathaniel Carnes to promote their sales of imported Chinese goods. She was then brought on tour by various managers who profited from her "exotic" presence. Every time Afong Moy appeared in exhibition, she was featured in a room of Chinese curiosities and dressed in native clothing and ornate accessories, her body constantly on the verge of disappearing into Oriental ornaments and colors. Her presence was confined to an imagined and generalized Chineseness, marked as a foreign Other. In her appearance, she disappeared, time and time again.

This chapter introduces TimeLine Theatre Company's (Chicago, IL) 2022 production of Lloyd Suh's *The Chinese Lady* (2018), a play that reimagines the life of Afong Moy beyond historical stereotypes.[3] TimeLine's version of *The Chinese Lady* paid careful attention to the playscript's calculated balance between history and fiction. The creative team brought the life of the past to its fullest animation by including a lobby display, program, and metatheatrical

DOI: 10.4324/9781032636337-8

frame that invited spectators to critically engage with the play's critique of archival absences, historiographic challenges, and the enduring nature of the Orientalist gaze. Written through the lens of my experience as the production dramaturg, this chapter describes how dramaturgs not only conduct historical research on *what* history is represented in the theatre but also critically engage with *how* theatre and performance inform history and vice versa. Working alongside the creative team, a dramaturg can function as a constructive curator, contextualizing the performance within history while conceptualizing and articulating a narrative of the present that acknowledges historical harm and seeks to address it.

When I began researching and writing for the dramaturgical packet, one central keyword soon surfaced: gaze. The repetition and variation of different gazes lie at the core of Suh's *The Chinese Lady*. The entire play takes place within the frame of continued performances spanning from 1834 to 1887, where the story is driven forward by the changing reception of "The Chinese Lady." Over several decades, the play captures how the public perception of China in the United States quickly evolved by tracing Afong Moy's treatment as a Chinese woman. As the play progresses, we witness a range of modes of scrutiny that Afong Moy experienced in her life—the curious gazes toward an "exotic" and admirable lady from a faraway land (scene 1), the stare of amazement toward the revered culture and history of China (scene 2), the voyeuristic gawking at her bound feet (scene 3), and the condescending looks that follow China's failure in the first Opium War (scene 4). Embedded within these modes of scrutiny are highly racialized and gendered preconceptions that conditioned Moy's marketing and reception in a US context. Through her analysis of images and representations of Asiatic femininity, Anne Anlin Cheng demonstrates how Asian women experience Orientalist gazes that reduce their existence to "ornamental artifice" (416). The danger of ornamental objectification looms in the backdrop of Suh's play, as he notes in the stage directions that Afong Moy should be dressed in decorative costume pieces and set in an "ornate" box "decorated with various types of Chinoiserie" (5). One of Afong Moy's lines reflects the playwright's awareness of the problem of viewing Asian women as ornamental surfaces. In scene 3, right before the critical moment when Afong Moy realizes people had been seeing her as less than human, she reveals her deepest hope: "to share more about who we are; not simply on the surface levels of clothing and adornments, but a deeper, more lasting intimacy" (21). The tragedy of Afong Moy lies in this gap between her vision of self and the reductive gazes directed at her. The play eventually culminates in Moy insisting that audiences participate in a collective examination of the politics of looking. She invites audiences to attend to their own gaze: "I'm looking at you," she says, "Are you looking at me?... Can you see me?" (41) These final questions might appear superfluous, as theatre is, quite literally, a place of seeing. What the questions imply, though, is that the act of looking is interpretive and bodes various possibilities of meaning. What the play works toward in the end is a sympathetic engagement with Moy that was never afforded her in history.

When I started my conversations with director Helen Young and the design team, the key question I posed was how our production could build a story arc about the various gazes. While the play demands that Afong Moy be dressed in ornamental surfaces and staged in a room of Chinoiserie, I encouraged the designers to find variations in each scene, showcasing how these gazes were historically specific to different times. This early dramaturgical identification of the gaze as a structural backbone to the play and our discussions of the importance of spectatorship later facilitated one of the major interventions in TimeLine's production. At the same time, I emphasized to the creative team the context in which we were producing this work, during the COVID-19 pandemic, in a moment of increased anti-Asian violence and sentiment. I asked: in our current context, how could our play truthfully represent the history of the Orientalist gaze without perpetuating it? This (re)consideration of what was at stake in our production guided our ongoing conversations.

For nearly thirty years, TimeLine Theatre Company has dedicated itself to "present[ing] stories inspired by history that connect with today's social and political issues" ("About TimeLine"). As a result, the company places a particular emphasis on the historical contextualization of productions and gives production dramaturgs support to create a rigorously researched lobby display and a behind-the-scenes magazine distributed to audience members at the theatre, *Backstory*. I invited viewers to recognize the play's historical specificity regarding the gazes that Afong Moy endured through several pieces in *Backstory*, the lobby display, and the website.[4] What's more, to provide our local audience members a recognizable point of access, my curated lobby display presented the history of Chicago's Chinatown as a pastiche of constructed Chineseness. The iconic attraction is indeed filled with ornamental surfaces and designs that were mostly replicated by Western architects who had never visited China before. The central message of the lobby display parallels an important revelation of the play—that in the US cultural imaginary, exoticized artifice is often equated with Asianness—to engage audiences with the play's local and historical questions before encountering the production itself.

In the very first scene of the play, Afong Moy directly reveals to the audience, "What is happening is a performance." She stresses, "For my entire life is a performance. These words that you hear are not my own. These clothes that I wear are not my own. This body that I occupy is not my own" (6). On the surface, the statement conveys how the white gaze imposes foreignness onto her body. At the same time, through Afong Moy, the playwright draws audience members' attention to the artifice of theatre: the living character is a mere illusion; she is but an actor, in costume, speaking the words of the playwright. By openly acknowledging this illusion, Suh's play differs from previous historical representations of Afong Moy, reimagining a degree of agency while naming Moy's inability to speak for and define herself on her own terms in the archival record. The play, indeed, strikes a careful balance between a need to recognize the historical erasure of Afong Moy and a desire to represent her as a real person with humor, thoughts, and feelings. In the words of Suh himself, the play is an attempt to "conjure and honor" Afong Moy, imagining her silent body with a voice of her own ("Personal Interview").

Building on my dramaturgical analysis of Suh's use of the gaze as a structural device and of the critical spectatorship written into the play text, the director eventually devised an original sequence that takes the play beyond its script. At our production, every evening before the show started, Mi Kang, who played Afong Moy in the production, sat still on the edge of the stage, in front of the drawn curtains. Dressed in a white tank top and blue jeans, she was not yet in the role of Afong Moy. As the audience members entered the theatre, she looked at everyone. Most of the audience members, however, would only briefly return her gaze, if they even looked at her at all. It was not until the curtains opened, when Mi Kang put on her Afong Moy costume and appeared as a character, that she received audiences' full attention. Dressed in native clothing and ornate accessories, she sat in a room filled with Chinese curiosities—just like Afong Moy in 1834. At the very end of the play, the actor, having been in the role of Afong Moy, took off her Chinese-style clothing, and once again revealed the white tank top and blue jeans underneath. As she walked to the very spot where she started the pre-show sequence, the room of curiosities also quickly traveled backward and disappeared in the dark. In this moment, she stood alone on a bare stage, leaving behind the fabric, ornaments, and curiosities that once defined her presence. Then, she invited the audience to "look at each other" (41). The house light slowly turned on. She said, "I'm looking at you," while exchanging looks with each audience member one after another. In this tender moment of sharing, the play ended with the actor asking her audience: "Are you looking at me? Can you see me?" (41). As discussed above, the final questions here demanded a focused encounter of the eyes—unmediated by the conventions of theatrical spectatorship—that suggests mutual recognition. The moment when a performer casts a long gaze at their spectators is fundamentally an act of resistance, redefining the power dynamics between the looker and the observed. The contemporary outfit extends the historical play into the present moment, acknowledging Afong Moy's story as emblematic of a past that continues to shape Asian American experiences today. This metatheatrical device reminds audience members that they have been watching a performance, and the entire performance is a collective reimagination of the past—a kind of critical spectatorship inherent in the script of *The Chinese Lady*. With the inserted pre-show sequence, audience members are offered an opportunity to reposition themselves in relationship to the history of objectified Asian bodies. In the end, when exhorted to return the gaze, spectators are invited to become active participants in a reenactment—but more importantly, a revision— of a historical encounter.

Driven by a dramaturgical attention to the porous temporalities and realities in the play, our production further anchored the performance in a liminal space where the past and present converge, and the real is intertwined with fiction. Occupying a curious ontological status between a contemporary actor and a historical character, the performer's body invited a multitude of possible identifications: in that final shared moment of looking, were we releasing Afong Moy from perpetual ornamental objectification? Or were we extending our recognition to the actor, and even contemporary Asian bodies in general? If anything, the heterogeneity of identifications counters the idea that meanings encoded in a specific racial body are historically predetermined and unchanging. It further suggests that the theatre can be a space where we involve ourselves in the production of counter-memory. In the end, TimeLine Theatre Company's production of *The Chinese Lady* was concerned with a larger question of theatre and history: anchored in the real happenings of the here and now, theatre has the power (albeit limited) to animate history with a life beyond the archive, making moments and creating new histories in present time—a power that a dramaturg's work can help to unleash.

Exercise

Conduct a scene-by-scene structural analysis of a play based on history. As you do so, attend to the playwright's historiographical approach: how does the playwright use historical materials in the play? How do they represent historical events and individuals? How do they handle historical unknowns or absences? To what extent does their approach to historiography and the representation of history govern the structure of the play and its meaning-making? The goal of this analysis is to identify (a) your sense of how the playwright is theorizing history and historiography and (b) how that theory is woven into the play itself at a structural and/or narrative level. Bring this analysis and your discoveries from it to your creative team early in the process, so it can inform critical creative decisions.

Notes

1 A version of the above first appeared in my dramaturgical essay for TimeLine Theatre. See Wu, "Afong Moy: The Chinese Lady," *The Chinese Lady, Backstory*, published by TimeLine Theatre Company, 2022. Reprinted with permission from TimeLine.
2 For a detailed account of Afong Moy's tours, see Davis, *The Chinese Lady: Afong Moy in Early America*.
3 Jiayi Chen and Maren Robinson have generously read earlier versions of this chapter, and I am grateful for their comments and suggestions.
4 Audience members were also provided with a QR code linked to an online lobby. The website featured additional resources and interactive content that were provided by the dramaturg: www.timelinetheatre.com/chinese-lady-lobby/

Works Cited

"About TimeLine." TimeLine Theatre Company, www.timelinetheatre.com/about/.

Cheng, Anne Anlin. "Ornamentalism: A Feminist Theory for the Yellow Woman." *Critical Inquiry*, vol. 44, no. 3, Spring 2018, pp. 415–46.

Davis, Nancy E. *The Chinese Lady: Afong Moy in Early America*. Oxford University Press, 2019.

Haddad, John. "The Chinese Lady and China for the Ladies: Race, Gender, and Public Exhibition in Jacksonian America." *Chinese America: History and Perspectives*, 2011, pp. 5–19. https://shop-chsa.square.site/product/h-p-2011/49?cp=true&sa=false&sbp=false&q=false&category_id=6.

Suh, Lloyd. Personal Interview. 7 April 2022.

Suh, Lloyd. *The Chinese Lady*. Dramatists Play Service, 2019.

Suh, Lloyd. *The Chinese Lady*. Directed by Helen Young, performed by Mi Kang and Glenn Obrero, production dramaturgy by Yiwen Wu, with assistance of Alisa Boland and Coco Wenke Huang, production by TimeLine Theatre Company, 8 May 2022–18 June 2022, Chicago.

The Chinese Lady, Backstory. Timeline Theatre Company, 8 May 2022, www.timelinetheatre.com/app/uploads/TimeLine_TheChineseLady_Backstory.pdf.

The Chinese Lady, Online Lobby. Timeline Theatre Company, 8 May 2022, www.timelinetheatre.com/chinese-lady-lobby.

7 "To Attach Our Floating Hearts"

The Dramaturgy of Queer Historiography

Percival Hornak

Dominant discourse often narrates the emergence of queer and trans people as a frightening new phenomenon. In response, one might search history for evidence that people with these identities have always existed and that, for this reason, they have a right to exist now. However, finding legible queer and trans historical figures is often fraught by rampant exclusion from the archive and narrow definitions of what counts as "queer" and "trans" that limit who *is* included. Often, queer people are written into history as friends, roommates, "gals being pals," or in other ways that obfuscate their identities either because they are not in control of what enters the historical record or because they conceal their queerness in order to survive. Instead of simply correcting the existing archive, we need to find new ways of writing history that disrupt the dominance of a record that structurally excludes queer and trans life. A turn to history by queer people is often motivated by the desire for a sense of community that stretches across time. Thus, for production dramaturgy supporting plays that engage with history, I propose a queer historiographic method that deprioritizes research oriented toward historical accuracy in favor of building affective connections across time between productions and the history they explore in order to redistribute the power to create historical records to queer and trans communities.

I employed this method as the dramaturg for a production of Sarah Ruhl's *Orlando* at the University of Massachusetts Amherst (US) in November 2022, directed by Iris Sowlat. *Orlando* tells the story of a nobleman and poet whose life spans five centuries and whose gender changes halfway through the story. Throughout, Orlando pursues a coherent sense of self only to conclude that she, in fact, contains a multitude of identities and that the *search* for meaning and concrete definition is more important than actually attaining it. This play's engagement with history is unique in its emphasis on multiplicity, imagination, and indeterminacy instead of accuracy and objective truth. Thus, it lent itself well to my queer historiographic dramaturgical method, which focused on building connections between the audience and the play's sense of history instead of attempting to educate the audience through rigorous historical research.

DOI: 10.4324/9781032636337-9

The scope of my dramaturgy for this production included proposing the script to a director and working with her to advocate for its inclusion in our university's season; collaborating on a specifically queer and trans lens for the production's design and casting concepts; and creating materials that could forge affective relationships between our production's artists and audience and the real lives of Virginia Woolf, Vita Sackville-West, and Violet Trefusis, which inspired Virginia Woolf's 1928 novel. Through our production, I wanted the artists and audience to find connections between their own lives and the lives of these historical figures as narrated in their letters, diary entries, and novels. These women are legible to us as queer in the present, but I was not particularly interested in using *Orlando* to teach about them. Rather, I wanted to engage the cast and audiences in an exploration of how traces of their tangled romances linger in our lives and communities today.

In my work on this production, I followed Carolyn Dinshaw's call for a way of doing queer history that is focused on forming affective relations across time, which in turn become the basis for building identity and community. She moves away from seeking causal connections between what came before and what exists now and toward forming relationships that inform the way we build communities in the present—a process that is deeply emotional and relational. Given that the historical record is often inaccurate when it comes to accounts of queer and trans life, I argue that a turn to the personal and the affective, to things often deemed inconsequential to narrations of the past, offers us a new way forward.

Theatre as an art form blurs what is real and what is fictional in its request for audiences to suspend their disbelief and respond to what they see onstage as though it were real, even though we arrive at a performance knowing that what we are about to see is pretend. Virginia Woolf grappled with a similar opposition in the practice of biography, attributing "granite-like solidity" to truth and "rainbow-like intangibility" to personality (149). The point of writing a biography is ostensibly to communicate the true events of a person's life, but representing their personality requires something more than listing facts. Woolf's "The New Biography" describes a method that blends fiction and truth in order to create something new, what she calls "that queer amalgamation of dream and reality, that perpetual marriage of granite and rainbow" (155). Woolf's advocacy for the necessity of including elements of fiction in our telling of fact goes hand in hand with thinking more deeply about the historical record and its constructedness—we cannot take for granted that it is true and complete, and we need to account as much for what is missing as we do for what has been preserved and recorded. Is "historical accuracy" a useful goal in this context? What does doing a play about queer history look like when queer and trans life in all their possible manifestations cannot be fully accounted for in the archive? I propose that we use the gaps we find as a starting point for imagining what might fill them and take on the writing of history ourselves.

Queer historiography takes up Foucault's concept of genealogy, which looks for the things that have been left out of dominant narrations. Instead of attempting to create a single continuous chain of historical events, genealogical approaches map history like constellations, finding links between different moments in time and making space for multiple narrations that can account for the subjectivity of memory and for the existence of unfillable gaps where we do not have a verifiable account of what happened. Ruhl's *Orlando* uses imagination (or, in Woolf's words, "rainbow") to fill such gaps and tell history playfully. A queer historiographic approach to dramaturgy for plays and productions that engage with history prioritizes building relationships between the actors and the subject matter that are rooted in the personal. It takes as its starting point the fact that accuracy is a slippery (if not impossible) goal for queer and trans history and asks what we might discover if we allow ourselves to use our imaginations in the telling of stories about the past. This method gives queer and trans communities the power to narrate their own histories in defiance of archives built to exclude them.

The dramaturgy for this production focused on making contact with the real people who inspired the play's characters, most notably Virginia Woolf, Vita Sackville-West, and Violet Trefusis. Actors had access to a digital whiteboard with information about the real-life people and places that are referenced in the play, with an emphasis on things that might give them touchstones or points of connection to their own lives. At our first rehearsal, I brought copies of letters and diary entries penned by these three central women for the cast and creative team to peruse and annotate in search of a passage that evoked some kind of significant emotional response for them, or that they found relatable. We shared our chosen sections, which led into a broader conversation about what it meant to do this play and to tell a story inspired by real people in history. This sharing asks a lot of the artists at the table and requires care on the part of the dramaturg who facilitates such conversations. It is crucial to take time to build trust and extend an invitation to share that genuinely can be refused should someone feel uncomfortable bringing their own experience to the material. In lieu of a roundtable conversation, one might also ask for writing on Post-it notes or similar lower-stakes ways of identifying connections to the story.

Actors whose characters directly corresponded to a real-life figure encountered obvious touchstones to draw from in their creative processes, but the group as a whole found points of connection that could lessen the distance between the 1920s, when Woolf wrote *Orlando: A Biography*, and 2022. Upon reading one of Vita's declarations of love in a letter to Virginia, the actor playing Orlando threw their head back and shouted, "I'm going to set myself on fire. When will someone do this for me?" This exercise used records penned by the queer women at the center of the play, but its goal was not to learn enough about these figures to accurately portray them onstage. The cast was empowered to decide for themselves what they wanted to focus on, which let them form a relationship with the history the play explores on their own terms instead of ones imposed by me as dramaturg. The feelings Vita, Virginia, and Violet were writing about felt so immediate and relatable to the cast; this sense of kinship across time created a foundation and a shared language from which we could craft the production.

These letters from our first rehearsal reappeared in an interactive lobby display—audience members could listen to recorded versions of the letters and leave notes to people they love on the lobby walls. This display was not trying to teach the audience what they need to know in order to understand what's happening in the play. Instead, it enacted a queer historiographic dramaturgy by encouraging audience members to get to know Vita, Virginia, and Violet and reflect on people to whom they might want to write their own letters. By leaving these love notes in the lobby, we created a historical record of sorts for our production: one that was simultaneously deeply personal and built communally. Rather than presenting the audience with lots of research about Woolf's novel and the different time periods in the play, I wanted us to displace that historical record in favor of our own, built from fragments of relationships and memories brought together by our production and grounded in the way these three central women narrated their own lives.

The overarching goal of queer historiographic work is to find history in unexpected places and to form affective connections across the ages that give us places to anchor ourselves. In Woolf's *Orlando*, as in Ruhl's adaptation, the title character grapples with his need for "something which he could attach his floating heart to" (Woolf 19). This guided all of the work I did for this production up to and including how the audience was welcomed into the theatre: a preshow playlist, which I created in collaboration with our sound designer, of contemporary trans and sapphic pop songs that connected dyke drama from a century ago to our lives today. This production created a link between Vita, Violet, and Virginia's historical moment and our own in a way that resonated with our cast, and with audience members who, inspired by Orlando's relationships, lingered in the lobby after performances to talk about their own. Instead of focusing on proving the existence of queer people in history, our production built a broader sense of community through shared emotional responses to the play and the story it tells about the past.

Engaging with queer history must go beyond searching for hard and fast evidence that queer and trans people existed in the past. The problem to be addressed is not that we believe we are some kind of new phenomenon, but instead that the way queer history tends to be narrated is sanitized of its feeling, and that figures with whom we might connect are missing. Those who cannot be assimilated into narratives of queer progress are left behind, guiding contemporary queer and trans people toward particular futures and casting aside figures who do not fit into the narrow arc of queer progress imagined by heteronormative culture. Enacting a queer historiographic approach to dramaturgy begins with choosing to produce plays that embrace the need for imagination to help animate historical fact and decentering the dramaturgs themselves as presenters of singular historical truth. The dramaturg instead serves as a facilitator for building relationships and identifying connections between the artists, audiences, and text.

This dramaturgical method opens up ways of using theatre's capacity for imagination and evoking feeling to form deep affective and emotional connections between queer and trans people and figures in the past. It activates what José Esteban Muñoz names as "a desire for another way of being in both the world and time, a desire that resists mandates to accept that which is not enough" (96). I encourage dramaturgs who work on plays about queer history to resist the urge to fix an archive that has erased and excluded queer and trans people in favor of building their own alongside the artists and audiences with whom they're working. While queer and trans communities experience some benefits from a more accurate historical record, I argue that we ought to look beyond simply correcting what exists and toward finding places to anchor our floating hearts and reclaiming the power to write history.

Exercise

This exercise builds personal relationships between the artists working on a production and the historical figures featured in the play. It works well in initial conversations with creative teams and actors.

1 Find a wide array of primary sources written by the historical figures present in your play—letters, diary entries, news articles, transcripts of speeches.
2 Print these primary sources out or make digital copies available to participants; it is important that they are able to write on or highlight them in some way. Unless you have a very large group or a small number of sources, you probably only need one copy of each.
3 Give participants time to sift through the materials you've gathered in search of a passage that evokes a noteworthy feeling for them. Encourage them to annotate as they go and to build on others' comments or highlights.
4 Have everyone share one quote that prompted a significant emotional response. As you facilitate this, try to steer folks toward how the texts made them feel and what connections they made to their own lives rather than what they learned about the historical figures.

Works Cited

Dinshaw, Carolyn. *Getting Medieval: Sexualities and Communities, Pre- and Postmodern.* Duke University Press, 1999.

Muñoz, José Esteban. *Cruising Utopia: The Then and There of Queer Futurity*. 10th Anniversary ed. New York University Press, 2019.

Ruhl, Sarah. *Chekhov's Three Sisters and Woolf's Orlando: Two Renderings for the Stage*. Theatre Communications Group, 2013.

Woolf, Virginia. "The New Biography." *Granite and Rainbow: Essays*. Girvin Press, 2012, pp. 149–55.

Woolf, Virginia. *Orlando: A Biography*. Harcourt, Brace, and Co., 1928.

Part II

New Play Dramaturgy

Staging History and Historiography

8 Staging the Queer Archive

soldiergirls in Process

Ryan Adelsheim

In May 1944, Esther Herbert, a twenty-one-year-old from Brooklyn and cadet in the Women's Army Corp (WAC), wrote to her first girlfriend, Marvyl Doyle:

> Honey it is Saturday, almost midnight and I am very sleepy—drowsy and I want to be with you nestled happily in your arms—fresh from a soapy bath with you. All clean and sweet and sleepy and you will make love to me 'cause I need it so and want it more so—everyday.
>
> (Herbert)

The two young women, separated by a military transfer, wrote to each other daily, but when Esther, lonely in San Bernadino, began an affair with Roberta (Bobbie), she broke things off with Marvyl. After the war, Esther and Bobbie remained in California, while Marvyl and her new girlfriend Sue moved to Florida to become teachers. Esther and Marvyl stayed in touch, and eventually, Esther convinced Marvyl and Sue to visit. When the two women saw each other for the first time in over a decade, they realized they were still in love. As they got back together, Bobbie and Sue struck up a relationship, and both couples lived in California, taking care of each other for the rest of their lives. It's all *so* gay.

Esther and Marvyl's letters, housed in the ONE Archives at the University of Southern California, serve as the raw material for *soldiergirls*[1]—a two-person musical comedy that retells Esther and Marvyl's love story and explores the formation of the WAC, its unlikely sparks of queer liberation, and the fracturing of gender expectations in the 1940s and today. There is an echoing familiarity embedded in this story—of queer women writing themselves into history, of lesbian drama, and of desire ringing across time. Queer historiographers see this familiarity as a desire for identification, one that both clarifies and occludes the past.[2] Scholar Heather Love reminds us that those same queer historical figures that spark positive identification hold a "backwardness," a refusal of modern attitudes toward queerness that accounts for the cost of homophobia (8–10). Love suggests that these backwards figures

DOI: 10.4324/9781032636337-11

Figure 8.1 Marvyl Doyle and Esther Herbert. Long Beach, CA, December 22, 1943. Courtesy of ONE Archives at the USC Libraries.

act on the present through a shameful or challenging identification, rather than merely an affirmative one (45, 35). By accounting for the still present pain, refusal, and marginality, Love argues that we might allow the queer archive to disrupt the present's march toward assimilation and create a more stable, more complete queer identity in the present. In short, we must allow the full range of experiences of the queer past to exist.

It was this tension between identification and refusal that drew us—Emil Weinstein, writer and director, and I, dramaturg and researcher—in. Initially inspired by Leisa D. Meyer's book, *Creating G.I. Jane: Sexuality and Power in the Women's Army Corps During WWII* (1998), we were fascinated by the nascent queer community emerging within the military. In the early days of the WAC, the institution swept accusations of lesbianism under the rug, quietly transferring suspected women rather than undesirably discharging them.[3] This policy inadvertently created a relatively comfortable space for queer women to find each other and form community for the first time. These connections would become the foundation of lesbian bar culture and the queer revolution of the 1950s–1970s (Gallo 150). The love stories and communities built during the war are not only familiar and entertaining but also crucial to creating queer futures. This chapter thinks alongside Clare Croft, Heather Love, and the queer archive to offer an approach to staging queer history that insists on a slippage between past and present. This strategy embraces the tension between historical accuracy and the desire for identification in an effort to put today's audiences and artists in direct contact with the queer past, allowing history to disrupt and inflect the present.

What we know about Esther and Marvyl's life together is held in photo albums, a brief 2006 interview with Herbert, and seemingly endless folders of letters—the intimate words of their epistolary relationship brimming with a new love and recognition as they found each other in the barracks of the WAC (Figure 8.2). Esther sends Marvyl wandering reports from her cross-country train trip, griping about the "flibberdigibit" women who aren't serving in the army and their families—"this trip is a study in how not to bring up children," she scribbles (Herbert). Her quotidian details mix with a pulsating desire, a kind of mid-twentieth-century sexting. Fewer of Marvyl's letters have been preserved, but she appears in photographs, and her voice surfaces through a collection of her poetry with titles like "Poem for E" and "Silver Band poem," which later became the basis for song lyrics in the show.

In her work on cultural critic Jill Johnston, Clare Croft (2021) describes the experience of lesbians in the archive:

> It is in the archive where—especially if one is looking for evidence of queer women's lives—one has to have tools to see what's there, what's not there, and all that might lie in the space between full presence and total absence. It is in this middle space where lesbians seem to live.
>
> (35)

Though neither Esther nor Marvyl publicly declared themselves lesbians, they represent a rare moment of queer archival speech, of full presence, standing in for so much absence. Even so, we need Croft's tools to see the struggle beneath their love story. Though their letters seem to reach into and ripple through a modern moment, during their time, the women were perched on a precipice of cultural transformation. Their lives were riddled with fear and secrecy as their unlikely intimacy formed within the violent, misogynistic military structure. With further research, Marvyl's lifelong struggle with depression comes to light, as does Esther's brief marriage to a man immediately after the war (during which she burned most of Marvyl's letters, worried about being discovered). Details buried in surviving letters suggest that they similarly struggle with their community, expressing veiled uncertainty about their friends' undesirable discharges and their own quiet shame. This intimate excavation of both invitation and refusal begs the question: how do we bring these figures that occupy an ambivalent, sometimes contradictory, position

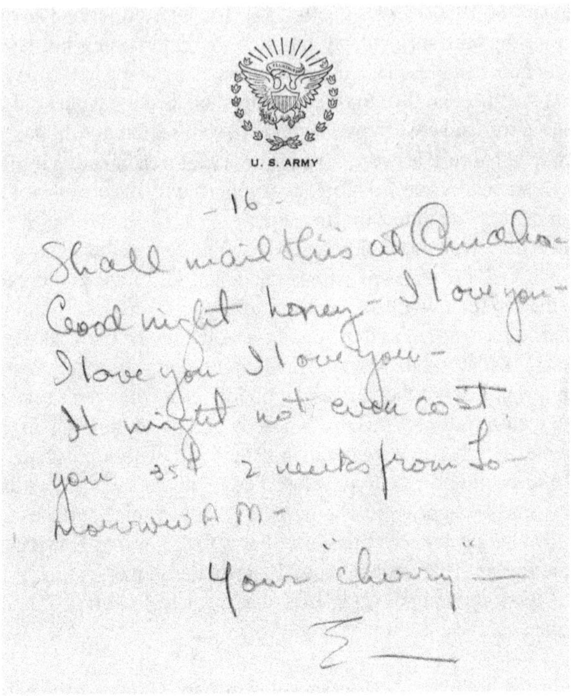

U. S. ARMY

-16-

Shall mail this at Omaha-
Good night honey- I love you-
I love you I love you-
It might not even cost
you 35¢ 2 weeks from to-
morrow A M-

Your "cherry"—
E—

Figure 8.2 Letter from Esther Herbert to Marvyl Doyle, February 20, 1944. Courtesy of ONE Archives at the USC Libraries.

between backwardness and recognizable front-footed queerness into a contemporary creative work?

After a 2019 archive visit, we embarked on a period of additional research and devising—transcribing and digitizing the letters we found most compelling to restructure into dialogue. At the same time, we researched the history of the WAC, experiences of queer WACs, postwar queer subcultures, popular music styles, and USO (United Service Organizations) shows of the time. With two skilled devising actors—Han Van Sciver and Madeline Seidman—and composer Emily Johnson-Erday, we began to build out Esther and Marvyl's love story and explore the social and political world around them. We embraced a citational and referential queer mode of operating: rather than eschewing our sparks of interest by conforming to a linear march through time, we focused on the places where we felt resonance, echoes, and hauntings of their story with our own and with related histories. Through this process, we dramatized the desire that queer historiographers identify—working to both represent these women based on the facts of the archive and build the affective space of recognition that cannot be accounted for in the historical record. The two actresses playing Esther and Marvyl meld into roles ranging from Colonel Oveta Culp Hobby, the first (and only) female Colonel in the army during World War II, to their fellow recruits, to the sexist army therapist, Major Albert Preston. The unfixity of their roles requires acting virtuosity, and their constant movement between power placements and genders dramaturgically underscores the women's precarious position as queer people in a new branch of the army. We enlivened a slippage of past and present by combining historical letters with a contemporary understanding of queerness through collage, citation, camp, and anachronism. For example, we paste a *Twelfth Night* monologue into Esther and Marvyl's meet-cute; speeches from opposing male senators devolve into a parody of phallic impotence; Marvyl shares a tongue-in-cheek pamphlet with Esther that teaches her—in a song—"How to Have Lesbian Sex"; and Marvyl's poems transform into a coffeehouse, girl-with-a-guitar sequence that plays on Riot Grrrl and Ani DiFranco musical styles.

By playing in these multivocal rhymes that emerge from queer subcultures (Halberstam 169–70), we engage in practices of queer adaptation, which Pamela Demory defines as an opening up of possibilities, a blurring of boundaries, and a promiscuity of perspectives that can bring a new awareness to the silences of dominant texts or, in this case, histories (2–4). *soldiergirls* makes these silences—better understood as Croft's middle space—visible in constructed moments of temporal slippage. These history-based characters have different language, musical scoring, or gaze than might have been true in 1944. We use their own words and add new vocabulary without denying their subjectivity. Instead, we demand to see their humanity, affinities, and constant becoming across time.[4]

In an entirely imagined scene early in their courtship, Esther and Marvyl shyly sit next to each other to watch a screening of the 1942 film *Now, Voyager*. Sound, light, and setting indicate that they are in a room full of fellow WACs. Perhaps the film is projected. Maybe we just hear its sound. They reveal that they both love the movie as they coyly whisper the lines along with the recording, and then suddenly, they are on their feet performing as Bette Davis and Paul Henreid in Charlotte and Jerry's climactic scene, stopping just short of the romantic kiss. Esther and Marvyl take on these roles to speak their unspeakable desire for each other. This multilayered process of recycling and revising embraces the backwardness of their lives—we transpose archival details about the fluttering uncertainty of their early flirtation into this scene where Esther and Marvyl claim another narrative as their own. Queer people are experts in imagining themselves inside love stories never meant for them. In the citational lip sync performance, they grow bigger and bolder than possible in their time. And yet, that gesture is stopped just short of consummation. They could never kiss in front of their entire squadron even in this moment of make-believe; the reality of their lives was too precarious.

At its essence, *soldiergirls* embodies the temporal contradiction of millennial artists taking 80-year-old intimate letters written in private for a lover and transforming them into the material of public performance. This process of extraction and editorializing is also one of fracturing and displacing: lines from letters turn into dialogue, snapshots turn into scenes, and stories from discrete oral histories are grafted onto characters' lives. In making a performance, reality (as we can glean it from the archive) and fiction blend. Motivating it all is the inextinguishable draw of familiarity—consciously and subconsciously, we underscore the moments that make us feel seen. We play right into Love's critique, rescuing what we like from history and allowing our affirmative bias to take center stage. And yet, stylistically, the show offers space for backwardness with comedy and a self-conscious embrace of lesbian camp. Comedy's capaciousness allows for tonal dissonance, contradiction, and irony in ways that serious drama often cannot. It allows pain to live on the surface and to be treated with frankness—rather than the quiet, tortured longing of so many white queer historical fictions, these characters can be direct. "I only sleep with girls," Marvyl brashly declares in another imagined scene (Weinstein 22). With a critical and political camp, *soldiergirls* holds both Love's critique and advocacy. Ann Pellegrini reminds us that camp "responds to the experience of homosexual stigmatization by sending up and theatricalizing the stigma, thereby ameliorating its impact" (170). *soldiergirls* engages in the manipulation of these stereotypes and political realities to connect to historical memory, to acknowledge stigmatized identity, and to "produce a different relation to the present and future" (Pellegrini 184).

We hope that when the loss and pain of the past collide with present-day theatrical vocabulary, the musical will not glibly push forward a progressivist narrative but will instead underscore how the patterns of the past continue to live in the present and equally how current codes of lesbian culture are themselves reflections of past practice. From the collision emerges a queer time, an intentional incongruity that reaches both backward and forward. Dramaturgically, engaging with the archive through queer staging and adaptation strategies allows us to see our past anew and strengthen our relationship with queer lineages.

Exercise

Queer Collisions

To find the places where queer voices might echo through time, try the following:

1 Spend some time researching the media your characters may have encountered. Make a list: What movies, plays, or novels were popular? What styles of music were mainstream, and which were underground? What are the contexts in which these characters consumed media? What mainstream

stories would they have made their own? What subcultures spoke directly to their experience?

2 Make a second list, this time doing some personal reflection: what were the pieces of media that spoke to you as you discovered your identity? What were the formative films, television shows, plays, and music for you?
3 Compare the two lists—what overlaps, intersections, and rhymes can you find? Begin working with these shared elements in the context of your larger story.

Notes

1 *soldiergirls* has received support from En Garde Arts, New York Theater Workshop, Rattlestick Theater, and The Mercury Store; the piece is in ongoing development. My thanks to Marc Robinson, Katherine Profeta, and the panelists and participants of QGrad 2021 for their generative feedback on drafts of this essay.

2 For more on the queer archive see Halberstam; Carolyn Dinshaw, *Getting Medieval* (Duke UP, 1999); Ann Cvetkovich, *Archive of Feelings* (Duke UP, 2003); and Tavia Nyong'o *Afro-Fabulations: The Queer Drama of Black Life* (NYU Press, 2019).

3 I use "undesirable" in deference to Leisa Meyer's work—this classification of dishonorable discharge stripped WACs of their veteran's benefits and marked these women as social misfits, not only their sexuality but their personhood deemed unwanted (Meyer 152, 171).

4 These ideas are deeply informed by scholars' work on queer time, including Halberstam; José Muñoz, *Cruising Utopia* (Duke UP, 2009); and Elizabeth Freeman, *Time Binds: Queer Temporalities, Queer Histories* (Duke UP, 2010).

Works Cited

Croft, Clare. "Not Yet and Elsewhere: Locating Lesbian Identity in Performance Archives, as Performance Archives." *Contemporary Theatre Review*, vol. 31, no. 1–2, April 2021, pp. 34–50. https://doi.org/10.1080/10486801.2021.1878504.

Demory, Pamela. "Queer/Adaptation: An Introduction." *Queer/Adaptation: A Collection of Critical Essays*, edited by Pamela Demory, Springer International Publishing, 2019, pp. 1–13. https://doi.org/10.1007/978-3-030-05306-2_1.

Gallo, Marcia M. "Organizations." *The Routledge History of Queer America*, edited by Don Romesburg. Routledge, 2018.

Halberstam, Jack. *In a Queer Time and Place: Transgender Bodies, Subcultural Lives*. New York University Press, 2005.

Herbert, Esther. Letters to Marvyl Doyle, 1944. Box 1, Folder 3. Coll2013–030 Esther Herbert and Marvyl Doyle Papers and Photographs, 1921–2011. ONE Archives at the USC Libraries, USC, Los Angeles, CA. 12 March 2019.

Love, Heather. *Feeling Backward: Loss and the Politics of Queer History*. Harvard University Press, 2007.

Meyer, Leisa D. *Creating GI Jane: Sexuality and Power in the Women's Army Corps during World War II*. Columbia University Press, 1996.

Pellegrini, Ann. "After Sontag: Future Notes on Camp." *A Companion to Lesbian, Gay, Bisexual, Transgender, and Queer Studies*, edited by George E. Haggerty and Molly McGarry. John Wiley & Sons, Incorporated, 2007, pp. 168–93.

Weinstein, Emil. *soldiergirls*. Unpublished, 2024.

9 Dancing Augmented Archives

Movement and Technology as Dramaturgical Practice

Al Evangelista

In this theatre, audience members face one another. The stage separates viewers into two opposing groups: audience members must make a choice about which side to sit on. Placed between them in the center of the alleyway stage, almost as if forgotten, stand balikbayan boxes with red bamboo mats on top. A dancer cautiously approaches a mat, brushes it smooth, lifts their hand, and places their hand on the mat, softly at first, and then with the weight and lean of their chest. As they shift their weight onto the box, sound reverberates into the space. When the dancer's hand is removed and their body leans back, the audio abruptly stops with the sound of a record scratch. Sound and gesture are linked. With another weighted press, we hear a brief phrase: "The exhibition is the first comprehensive display of the Filipinos." And then, the announcement stops with another record scratch. Movement in this performance activates archival sound: analysis and descriptions of people from the Philippines on display at the 1904 St. Louis World's Fair. Some historians and archivists describe what happened at the 1904 World's Fair as a "human zoo," others, as "human exhibits." What matters is that these people "on display" faced impossible choices. What matters is that this exhibit was rooted in the racist practices of eugenics. In this theatre, dancers—their bodies and their weight—bring these archives into performance. This chapter explores my artistic direction and dramaturgy for *somewhere good*, which intentionally problematizes such archives relevant to anti-racism practices via choreography and augmented reality (AR).[1]

somewhere good, an evening-length dance theatre performance, originally debuted at Oberlin College with a cast of undergraduates. Through research, embodied exploration, and contextualization of the history of violence at the 1904 World's Fair, *somewhere good* invites audiences to engage with this complex history in a way that encourages anti-racist practice through the questioning of popular representations of Filipinx and Filipinx-American histories and narratives. The production utilizes movement, technologically embedded archival artifacts, and a focus on marginalized voices to offer a counternarrative to

DOI: 10.4324/9781032636337-12

Figure 9.1 Jewel Cameron, dancer, activates sound by pressing the balikbayan box. © John Seyfried

dominant discourses of anti-Asian hate and invite audiences to consider postcolonial critiques of this period of Asian American history.

While this writing is focused on a specific case study, my hope is that it will provide insight into the ways in which performance dramaturgy, combined with augmented reality, can be used to interrogate historical and contemporary issues of violence and injustice. By foregrounding the dramaturgical methods and techniques of ambiguity and care used in *somewhere good*, I aim to provide one potential guide for artists and scholars interested in using performance to address similar issues. Theorists know that performance has the potential to generate new knowledge and new understandings; embodied methods of inquiry can help us recognize and respond to the ongoing struggle against anti-Asian hate and other forms of systemic violence. However, like the act of theorizing, this engagement with historical narratives will always be limited and may pose risks of harm as histories are reinscribed on living bodies. How can performance address this violence? The dance dramaturgy I employ here and propose as a counter to anti-Asian narratives and historical erasure foregrounds ambiguity and care as feminist praxis. With the resurgence of anti-Asian hate alongside the COVID-19 pandemic, many Asian American historians, academics, activists, and artists find ourselves repeatedly conveying a depressing fact—anti-Asian hate is not new (Kwan and Wong; Baldoz). From indentured workers and human zoos to hate crimes and threats against Nobel Prize winners, violence against Asians and Asian Americans has been prevalent throughout US history and proliferates today.

How can this persistence and continuation of anti-Asian hate be forgotten or intentionally ignored?

For instance, three hundred years after Spanish colonization, the Philippines did not gain independence but instead became a US territory. As a means of justifying this new colonization, the United States began a misinformation campaign describing how the United States and its citizens were "graciously saving" the Philippines. Part of this political agenda and narrative was advanced by the 1904 World's Fair exhibit, which "curated" people from the Philippines and displayed them as uncivilized others to demonstrate why this rescue was necessary. The archives of the 1904 World's Fair recreate this colonial curation. The archives overwhelmingly center colonizer perspectives. As a result, they fail to critique the World Fair exhibit's impact on its participants and spectators, the exhibit's influence on anti-Asian racism today, and the exhibit's popularization of anti-Asian stereotypes used as propaganda that remain in circulation. *somewhere good*'s performance uses weight-activated audio and an augmented reality app operated by audience members to explore how to remember this traumatic history and how to continue to move with and against its absences, its forgettings, and the ongoing practices of anti-Asian hate.

In the first act, dancers move within the alleyway stage, reaching toward some invisible presence above, manipulating unseen objects, and reacting to unseen forces. The dancers run searching for unidentifiable things underneath the audience members' seats while also dodging an invisible wall onstage. In the second act, all the movements are the same, repeated exactly as the first. However, the audience is encouraged to use QR codes printed on the balikbayan boxes to access an augmented reality website through which they will view the second act of the performance. Using this AR, audience members—through their mobile devices—are finally able to see what the dancers are avoiding, sliding under, and running around. The invisible wall that shaped the dancers' movement reveals itself as a wall of historical texts and shapes, drawn from the 1904 World's Fair archives. The choreography, a mix of ambiguous gestures performed to synth-pop beats and recordings of archival text, remains open to multiple interpretations. There is still an element of something missing, but this incoherence is central to the piece's dramaturgy. The moral and evidentiary ambiguity of historical research in problematic archives is recreated for audiences through the purposefully unstable and indeterminate augmented reality interface.

Part of the dramaturgical problem here, especially when working with a flawed archive rampant with anti-Asian racism and pointedly omitting the voices of Asians and Asian Americans themselves, is finding a way to communicate those flaws without perpetuating harm. Augmented reality offers one solution to reveal what is there but not seen what can be felt but remains invisible. To avoid imposing a singular lens on the experience, the movement itself and the augmented reality remain fragmented, a parallel of the archive itself. This can feel frustrating, confusing, or maybe even boring, but that is the point. The dramaturgical intervention, here, is to draw audiences' attention to and invite them to dwell in the ambiguity and discomfort inherent to working in such archives. The work purposefully withholds text via AR in order to leave audience members with more questions than answers. Dramaturgically, I see this withholding as an invitation. This invitation—to unknowns and things unseen—manifests in moments that others might consider failure. For example, the performance does not clearly signal which aspects of Filipinx-American identity are being explored onstage. By refusing to make those elements more transparently legible, the performance parallels the lived experience of choosing when and where to make historically marginalized aspects of one's identity visible and to whom. In its insistence on ambiguity, the piece issues a provocation: "How do we cultivate curiosity about histories that will always remain unknowable? How do we learn to embrace the unknown? How might dwelling in the unknown produce its own forms of knowledge?"

The piece's dramaturgical ambiguity moreover manifests in the proliferating ways in which an audience might engage with the work. The audience is given choices: which side to sit on and when to (dis)engage with the AR and the choreography. The strategy, as a dramaturgical approach, was to cultivate audiences' ability to make choices with limited information and to sit with the difficulty and frustration that might result. While this might seem to encourage audiences to accept defeat, I saw it as a way of cultivating audiences' resilience in the face of seemingly debilitating ambiguity. Perhaps most importantly, *somewhere good* incorporates a politics of tenderness into its dramaturgy. The dramaturgical research and developmental process foregrounded care in honoring the stories of Filipinx World's Fair participants as accurately as possible given the limited information available. This approach, originating from a Black feminist performance praxis, emphasizes vulnerability and softness as critical components. Rather than imposing a definitive imagined counternarrative to archival absences, the production's invitation to dwell in uncertainty challenges notions of resistance that seek merely to reverse existing power dynamics. Ambiguity informed by a politics of tenderness offers an alternative vision of what it means to resist and survive in the face of systemic violence.

The title of the work, *somewhere good*, honors this dramaturgical strategy of embracing the unknown with tenderness. It comes from an Instagram Q&A with poet Ocean Vuong.[2] A fan commented that, like Vuong, they had recently experienced the loss of their mother and that they had found healing and connection in Vuong's poetry. Vuong's reply was one of unsurprising radical empathy and mutual support. He expressed his own profound grief and lack of answers yet described finding solace in their shared experience and articulated a hopeful wish that their mothers were in a better place. The original working title of this performance also took a phrase from Vuong's poetic response, which emphasized connection through pain. However, after

Figure 9.2 Mid-performance screenshot of *somewhere good*'s augmented reality interface. © Al Evangelista

dramaturgical analysis and research at the University of Michigan's Library of Special Collections, I could not justify the way the title overly foregrounded pain rather than inquiry and vulnerability. As I conducted my research at the University of Michigan's Special Collections, I repeatedly discovered items justifying narratives of colonization and was confronted with the absence of Filipino/a/x voices. At the same time, instead of supporting Filipinx-American healthcare workers, who were dying at a disproportionate rate from COVID-19, Americans increasingly and alarmingly espoused anti-Asian hate (Escobedo et al.). Because of this, I shifted the focus of the title from pain and wounding to one of hope and healing. *somewhere good* as a revised title gestures toward the absences and unknowns inherent in this performance work. The title also works to honor the missing and what is lost, instead of focusing on past and recurring trauma. In my dramaturgy of the show, including my historical research, structuring of the work, and inclusion of AR, I chose to focus on the potential and what else might be.

This type of work offers one example of how performance can create space for interrogating and challenging anti-Asian hate through dramaturgical research and practice. Using an approach rooted in anti-hegemonic, queer, and Black feminist praxis, the production contextualizes the history of violence against Asians and Asian Americans while also inviting audiences to engage with this history viscerally and emotionally. The incorporation of technology through an augmented reality app underscored the choreography's investment in recognizing the limits of our ability to access and understand the past, even as we honor the lived experiences of individuals underrepresented in the archive. Stories like these are never finished, and our perspectives on them are always changing. Maybe bodies in motion can help us write anew.

Exercise

If you were to consider using invisible text onstage during your show, where would it be, what would it say, and how could performers move alongside, against, and with that text? In what other ways might the invisible text impact the playing space and the world of the performance? How could this invisible text draw attention to the limits of our knowledge? How might AR or projection be used to productively make this text partially or temporarily visible to audiences?

Notes

1 The author would like to thank Kevin McDonald, Caitlin A. Kane, and Erin Stoneking for their generous edits and thoughts on the drafts of this work. All errors are my own. A version of this chapter was presented at the ASA 2023 Conference and the AAAS 2024 Conference.

2 Instagram, November 28, 2021, https://www.instagram.com/ocean_vuong.

Works Cited

Baldoz, Rick. "The 'Bad Day' Defense after the Atlanta Shooting Reinforced the Idea of White Victimhood." *The Washington Post*, 26 March 2021, https:// www.washingtonpost.com/outlook/2021/03/26/bad-day-defense-after-atlanta-reinforced-idea-white-victimhood/.

Escobedo, Loraine A., Brittany N. Morey, Melanie D. Sabado-Liwag, and Ninez A. Ponce. "Lost on the Frontline, and Lost in the Data: Covid-19 Deaths among Filipinx Healthcare Workers in the United States." *Front Public Health*, vol. 10 (2022), p. 958530. https://doi.org/10.3389/fpubh.2022.958530.

Evangelista, Al. "somewhere good." Live Performance, May 20 and 21, 2022.

SanSan Kwan, Yutian Wong. "Dancing in the Aftermath of Anti-Asian Violence: An Introduction in Three Parts." *Conversations Across the Field of Dance Studies*, vol. 42, 2023, pp. 1–15.

10 Animating Loss

The Role of Historiography in New Play Development

Erin Stoneking

"The Dotts Johnson Project," supported by The University of Alabama's Collaborative Arts Research Initiative (CARI), drew together an interdisciplinary team of collaborators (Robin Behn, Luvada A. Harrison, Yolanda Manora, Claudia Romanelli, and myself) to research the life and career of under-recognized African American actor, singer, and composer Hylan Montaqu "Dotts" Johnson[1] and make his work legible and accessible to scholars and the public.[2] Johnson's granddaughter, Harrison, a vocal artist herself, initiated the project to reclaim his legacy for herself and for future generations of her family. From the project's inception, we determined that one of the central modes of communicating our findings would be an original musical, *The Moods of Dotts Johnson in Song*, co-written by the group and featuring Harrison as a performer.[3] The musical features songs drawn from Johnson's known repertoire, including his original compositions, arranged by composer Etienne Charles.

With no formal biographies of Johnson, scant scholarship treating his career, and few archival resources to draw on, the creative team (on which I served as development dramaturg, researcher, and co-creator) found ourselves engaged simultaneously in the efforts of historiography (that is, gathering and critically synthesizing archival materials to write a history) and dramatization of that history. *The Moods of Dotts Johnson in Song*, in its concurrent development with archival research efforts, came to drive and feed that research just as the research shaped the musical theatre piece. The processes of historiography and new play development, in other words, more than inextricable, were mutually constitutive, troubling linear models of history-based play development that figure the playwriting process as one of translation or adaptation of accepted historical narrative into dramatic form. This symbiotic project model propelled me to attend to and elaborate on how these processes were co-determining, as part of the resulting musical itself.

Following the work of Saidiya Hartman in negotiating the tensions inherent in "against the grain" historiographical efforts which are "enmeshed with the relations of power and dominance that [they] striv[e] to write against" (*Scenes of Subjection* 11), *The Moods of Dotts Johnson in Song* strives "both

DOI: 10.4324/9781032636337-13

to tell an impossible story and to amplify the impossibility of its telling" ("Venus in Two Acts" 11). In an attempt to acknowledge and openly grapple with the limitations of dramatization and (via Hartman) critical fabulation in yielding closure to or recovery of the past within the play itself, I proposed that we adopt "animating loss" as a guiding dramaturgical principle in our writing process. For me, as a dramaturg working with a team of collaborating writers, the principle bore the additional benefit of creating a shorthand for a standard that helped me navigate moments in which there were differences of opinion around how to proceed with a particular beat or scene: does the proposed dramatic moment, ultimately, adhere to the concept of "animating loss"? Will that "animating loss" register with audiences? By outlining the development of the principle and some of the ways we implemented "animating loss" in writing the musical, I hope to demonstrate that recurrence to this standard might offer a more broadly applicable approach to dramatizing the role of historiography in developing new, history-based work for the stage and for rendering transparent historiography's processes and limitations.

Born in Baltimore in 1913 to working-class parents, Dotts Johnson knew from a young age that he wanted a life in the performing arts. Dissatisfied with the dearth of creative opportunities in Jim Crow Baltimore, Johnson left home at sixteen and headed North to Harlem. Once there, he began singing in nightclubs and supported himself with odd jobs before enrolling with the American Negro Theatre's School of Drama in 1945, which brought him into the orbit of some of the leading Black theatre artists of the 1940s–1960s, including Alice Childress, Sidney Poitier, and Canada Lee. His big break was a star turn in Roberto Rossellini's landmark film *Paisan* (1946). Johnson played an African American military policeman who fantasizes about the celebratory welcome he will receive upon returning to the United States after an Allied victory before ultimately grappling with the reality that a homecoming in fact promises a return to the same poverty and anti-Black racism that conditioned his life prior to military service. The film was critically acclaimed, garnering top prizes on the national and international film circuits, and launched Johnson into the public eye. Yet, as contemporaneous profiles and interviews in the Black press attest, he found himself living out a similar dissonance to the character he played: Johnson struggled to reconcile his newfound international celebrity with the lack of substantial roles available to him as a Black actor in the United States in the 1940s–1950s. Through his writing, public commentary, and forthright rejection of demeaning roles, Johnson contributed to the discourse around Black artists and representation over his ensuing career, which spanned stage, radio drama, live music, music composition and recording, television, and film. Johnson's politics and experiences were a major influence on his life partner, white Canadian actress and activist Madeleine Sherwood, best known as a character actress in Tennessee Williams's plays and "Mother Superior" in the *Flying Nun* television series. The couple's romantic relationship spanned from 1950 until his death in 1986.

When the teenaged Johnson left home in 1930, he left behind an infant daughter, Monterey, whose own daughter, Luvada Harrison, would go on to forge a career path in some ways eerily resonant with Johnson's. Harrison grew up in post-Civil Rights Baltimore, bused from her predominantly Black neighborhood into a white school where music classes were offered. Harrison cultivated a deep love of vocal performance and honed her talents in her local church and university program before heading to New York City in pursuit of a career in opera. Feeling caught between a sense of skepticism from Black friends and family who regarded opera as a monolithically white art form and the failure of US opera companies to implement inclusive casting practices, Harrison found a symbolic and artistic home in Italy and the Italian language. Growing up, she was only vaguely aware of her grandfather's career: she knew that he had, at one time, achieved some fame as a film actor, though she did not know he was a stage actor, musician, and composer. He sent her letters, occasionally, or political pamphlets; she visited him at his Harlem apartment as a child. They never discussed his artistic work. After his death in 1986, Harrison was the only family member in New York City and was delegated by Harrison's mother and a distraught Sherwood to clear out his cluttered apartment. Harrison sifted through his belongings, collected over decades, and duly meted them out to friends or discarded them, keeping only a small assortment of objects that sparked her interest.

It was only years later, as a professor at the University of Alabama, that a chance conversation facilitated through a CARI event with a colleague and scholar of Italian neorealist film (Romanelli) would set Harrison on a quest to learn more about her grandfather. Loss animates the musical first and foremost through Harrison's loss of her grandfather: as Harrison learned more about her grandfather's artistic practice, she felt more keenly the enormity of his loss both as a family member and as an artistic ancestor. Our research sought to temper Harrison's personal loss to the extent possible, and more broadly to rectify the loss of knowledge represented by the lack of scholarship treating Johnson's work. New and sometimes unanswerable questions emerged as we pieced together the sometimes literally marginal traces of Johnson in performing arts historical collections. Concomitantly, questions that arose while developing Johnson as a character ("How did he travel from Baltimore to Harlem? What did his parents think of his work in the theatre?") sent me back to the archive. I kept a journal in which I recorded the questions and unknowns generated by both our writing sessions and the archival research. At the beginning of each new writing session, I began by reading selections of these to the group (occasionally, with reports on developments from the research), both as a way of drawing us back into the flow of writing and as a way of foregrounding the methods and process of historiography and its limitations.

In the moments—familiar to scholars working with historically marginalized subjects in the archive—in which we found ourselves fruitlessly following even the most improbable trails through far-flung collections in search of a mere mention of Johnson, I asked the team to grapple with how to address those unknowns, the absences in what has been recorded and preserved. To what extent could we responsibly imagine answers to our unanswered research questions on the stage? And how could we convey the complexity and ambiguity of this research and development process as part of the musical itself, asking our audiences to reckon with the possibility that we may never fill some of the archival gaps? "Animating loss," as a dramaturgical principle, thus describes the ways in which the personal and historical dimensions of loss drive the play and the development of the play, but also underscores the commitment to putting that loss in motion onstage, pointing back to it in order to illuminate the processes of historiography. The title of the musical itself is emblematic of this approach: it is drawn from promotional material created by Johnson for a musical program with the same title, which may have been offered in conjunction with a planned personal appearance tour. We have been unable to locate any information regarding the tour or the contents of the program. The adoption of the musical program's title for our own project gestures toward the way archival absences structure the piece, even as the piece strives to redress Johnson's relegation to relative obscurity within popular and scholarly performing arts histories. It is also emblematic of "animating loss" as a dramaturgical approach: I worked actively to identify the historical gaps and regularly presented them to the creative team, encouraging us to embrace them as the constitutive material of the musical, rather than regard them as dramatic holes to be filled.

Although Harrison had always intended to perform in the musical, attending to her personal loss as an animating force in both the research and the dramatization clarified for the writing team the necessity of including her as not just a character but the central character of the piece; it also suggested a structure that reflected the fits and starts of our research. The character Luvada's story plays out contrapuntally with Dotts's, unsettling a totalizing historical account by foregrounding the contemporary process of research and the questions that remain unanswered. The resulting plot resists a linear progression of time and narrative that might map neatly onto an Aristotelian structure and ultimately provides no clear climax or resolution. Though the character Luvada may end the play knowing more about her grandfather than she does in the opening scene, the prevailing sense—undermining the disjointed unfolding of Johnson's biography—is one of uneasy stasis. This stasis is apparent in the mirroring of the opening and final scenes, in which Luvada sorts through Dotts's belongings in his Harlem apartment, following his death. Opening and closing the play with the packing up of the newly lost Dotts's apartment also underscores the site as both the source of much of the historical evidence remaining to us (the few items Harrison kept have been instrumental in guiding our research in other, more formal repositories) and the source of a secondary and profound loss. Uninformed about the expanse and import of Johnson's work and stretched for storage space in her own tiny New York City apartment, Harrison had no way of contextualizing his personal archive or of preserving it in the long term. Repeatedly, in our research and in the development of the musical, we have returned to this lost archive and what it contained or might have contained. In identifying this recurrence and drawing it under the principle of "animating loss," I suggested to the creative team that the apartment archive presented an important opportunity to dramatize both the processes of historiography and the losses at the heart of the musical. As a result, the musical begins and ends in the apartment, and, indeed, never truly leaves it: the intervening scenes play out, with other settings suggested by the addition of a table or bench, against the backdrop of the profusion of objects in Dotts's apartment.

Without this personal archive, our historical research often relies upon the Black press (such as *Jet* and *The New York Amsterdam News*), letters and production records from collections related to Black artists who worked with Johnson, and, more problematically, the writings of white critics, directors, and playwrights, and the papers of his partner Madeleine Sherwood. In our writing sessions, I prompted the creative team to consider this aspect of "animating loss" in developing the character of Madeleine. While Sherwood's reflections on Johnson are imbued with her deep love for him, in the absence of other accounts of his personal and interior life (including, most significantly, his own), her perspective becomes a primary lens through which he appears as a character. The character Madeleine is thus included in the musical not just because she is an important figure in Dotts's life, but because it allows us to dramatize how our existing historical evidence is conditioned and limited. Following Dotts's death, Madeleine remains Luvada's only connection with her grandfather; much of what Luvada knows about him originates in Madeleine's conversational and written anecdotes about him.

Finally, the musical establishes a convention of direct address for Luvada early on, often deployed in conjunction with the projection of archival material. These Brechtian elements are not bent toward establishing narrative authority through reference to historical evidence but instead allow us to call into question the basis for historiographic authority, given the ideologically inflected and incomplete nature of the archive. Luvada's direct addresses provide a frank metacommentary on what we can and cannot know or recover about her grandfather and how we have located what we do know. In the process, this metacommentary lays bare the mundane practices, decipherments, and frustrations that characterize archival work—labor that is often popularly romanticized as a kind of rarefied treasure hunt.

Exercise

As you conduct archival research in support of a production or new work, keep an exhaustive list or journal of the unanswered questions, deadends, or rabbit holes that arise as part of your research process. Periodically review the list and consider:

1 How might this list inform or emerge in the play (structure, dialogue, action, setting, characters)?
2 How might this list manifest in production (rehearsal processes and materials, staging, public-facing dramaturgical materials)?

Notes

1 In addition to the other archival challenges noted in this chapter, Johnson used multiple spellings of his nickname and given name throughout his career. I will default to "Dotts" as it is the spelling and name he used in the latter half of his life.

2 This project is also supported in part by the National Endowment for the Arts and The University of Alabama's Departments of Gender and Race Studies and Modern Languages and Classics. As of this writing, the play has had one developmental workshop reading. A second workshop is planned for Fall 2024.

3 For the sake of clarity, I use the names "Johnson," "Sherwood," and "Harrison" in reference to the people, and "Dotts," "Madeleine," and "Luvada" in reference to the dramatic characters.

Works Cited

Hartman, Saidiya V. *Scenes of Subjection: Terror, Slavery, and Self-Making in Nineteenth-Century America.* Oxford University Press, 1997.

Hartman, Saidiya V. "Venus in Two Acts." *Small Axe*, vol. 26, 2008, pp. 1–14.

Johnson, Dotts, actor. *Paisan* [*Paisà*]. Federico Fellini Organizzazione Film Internazionale in collaboration with Foreign Film Productions, 1946.

11 Dramaturgy of Internal Displacement in Nigeria

Elaigwu P. Ameh

Anybody anywhere can become displaced at any time. An individual is not *born* but, rather, *becomes* an internally displaced person (IDP). Rather than view displacement as a problem of the Global South or any other section of humanity, we need to see it as a human phenomenon. It can happen to any of us irrespective of our ethnicity, nationality, race, religion, gender, political affiliation, or socioeconomic status.[1] A major difference between IDPs and refugees is that, although refugees and IDPs are persons fleeing persecution or disaster, refugees have crossed the international borders of their countries, while IDPs are on the run within the borders of their own country and remain under the protective control of their home government, even if the government is overtly or covertly the cause of their displacement.

In this chapter, I reflect on the dramaturgical techniques that I implemented while crafting *Displaced*, an ethnographic performance created with IDPs. These techniques allowed the performance to reflect the cartographies of power at play in the relationships among IDPs, and between IDPs and humanitarian actors—relationships that drastically affect the variety, quantity, quality, and regularity of the aid IDPs receive. Such techniques provide new insights into our understanding of the players, scripts, and publics involved in the lives of IDPs. They also evidence how performance can assist in creating and conscientizing the micro-publics needed to tackle issues surrounding IDPs and humanitarian actors. This work demonstrates how a dramaturg can—and indeed does—make more legible and accessible the conceptualization, co-creation, and staging of embodied histories of persons or groups historically marginalized.

The overall aim of my research was to understand and share the lived experiences of displaced persons in Nigeria, with a view to providing an effective space for uncovering silences and forging alliances geared towards bettering the lives of this vulnerable population. This research largely took place in Bakassi IDP camp in Borno State and Durunmi IDP camp in Abuja, between June 2017 and May 2019. The IDPs were all from northeast Nigeria and had been displaced because of incessant attacks by the Islamic terrorist group, Boko Haram. During the conduct of my research, the Bakassi camp housed

DOI: 10.4324/9781032636337-14

over thirty-five thousand IDPs, while the Durunmi camp had a population of a little over two thousand.

The major components of this on-site research included participant observation, interviews, story circles, theatre improvisation workshops, and self-reflexive drama projects. In the recruitment of research participants, I employed face-to-face public invitations. I took a walk through the camps, moving from tent to tent, seeking participation in the research project. I combined this approach with the snowballing technique, which involved interviewees recommending other individuals for participation in the project. I complemented this effort with a sampling for range which, as a dramaturgical technique, allowed for identifying and interviewing subcategories of IDPs relevant to the study, namely young men and women, elderly men and women, single men and women, and married men and women—all of them between the ages of 18 and 65. The research happened in three phases.

During the first phase, I spent my time in IDP camps in Borno and Abuja, observing and recording the lived experiences of IDPs in these camps, their relations among themselves, and their interactions with humanitarian actors. A grant from the Office of Engagement Initiatives at Cornell University made this recruitment possible. With the help of thirteen research assistants, I conducted 673 interviews. The first phase of the research culminated in story circles: a group of people who tell stories about their own personal experiences following a prompt by a facilitator. I facilitated twelve story circles with IDPs, with six sessions being entirely for men and the other six entirely for women. Breaking the story circles into groups, using gender as a parameter, was another dramaturgical technique I employed to elucidate the intricacies of gender differentiation among IDPs and to amplify the needs, skills, perspectives, and influence of internally displaced women. The technique also assisted me in cross-fertilizing and consolidating information already gleaned from participant observation and interviews about gender-related concerns of IDPs, further underscoring the overlooked fact that IDPs are not a homogenous group and that internal displacement affects them disproportionately, with women and children suffering the most. Women in Northern Nigeria have habitually faced religious, cultural, and socioeconomic inequalities. Internal displacement worsens these preexisting inequalities and deepens the vulnerabilities of female IDPs. In addition to competing with male IDPs for limited job opportunities in the host community, female IDPs often face exploitation by security and aid agents and oppression by male IDPs.

The second phase of my field research was collective theatrical creation. I tapped into my expertise as a playwright-dramaturg to facilitate theatre improvisation workshops. In this phase of the research, I leveraged indigenous performance practices such as dance, folklore, proverbs, and music not just to increase interest among IDPs in the project but also to accentuate their agency and voice as co-participants in the collective theatrical creation. My participation in the theatrical creation was as much that of a dramaturg as it was that of a playwright, as is frequently the case when working on plays collectively created. The writing of this play constitutes its own form of writing history from below, not just because it centers the perspective, agency, and voices of IDPs themselves, but because it allows IDPs as ordinary people to construct and narrate their (hi)stories. This dramaturgical technique of co-creating (hi)stories from below allows IDPs to become not just storytellers but historians as well, as they promote new perspectives on their past and demonstrate how their past is relevant to the(ir) present and the(ir) future. It offers IDPs a chance to take ownership of their lived experiences and contribute meaningfully to ongoing discussions about the history of internal displacement in Nigeria, while also questioning some of the naïve and worrying assumptions about IDPs in the country and beyond.

The dramaturgy of internal displacement essentially involves centering the voices of IDPs in decision-making processes that concern them. True to this dramaturgy, even while serving as a scribe for all the story circle groups, I listened to and wrote down the priorities of IDPs on flowcharts. I reminded myself that I was not writing my story but theirs, and what they wanted written would be my focus. Prioritizing the needs of IDPs was an incredibly revealing exercise: there was a consensus on what constituted the needs of IDPs, but the consensus did not extend to what mattered most to all IDPs. While, for some IDPs, food security topped their list of needs, for many others, housing, resettlement, or a return to their homes was their top priority. A few were most concerned about the educational future of their children and were highly vocal about the need for quality education. All of them, however, affirmed the need to end the conflict that caused their displacement, even though some of them openly expressed skepticism about the swiftness of any end to the crisis since, according to them, the crisis had already evolved into a cash cow for the political class, security agencies, and non-state humanitarian actors in the country. Nevertheless, after protracted back-and-forth discussions, we came up with a list of key issues to include in *Displaced*. In writing the script for *Displaced*, I made sure to include certain harrowing experiences that some IDPs insisted should be part of the play. These experiences included child malnutrition, poor sanitary resources for women, camp officials' sex-for-food schemes, the re-bagging and sale of food supplies meant for IDPs on the black market, the forced sex between humanitarian actors and female IDPs, and the perennial food insecurity in the camp. Recurring themes in my interactions with IDPs also gained prominence in the play. To grant anonymity to the IDPs, I omitted their names and other personal identifiers that could give them away.

As a scribe, one of my dramaturgical strategies was to reflect on the cartographies of power at play among IDPs, and between IDPs and humanitarian actors. From my reflection, I gathered, for instance, that one of the roles new IDPs quickly learned when they got into the camp was submissiveness to camp officials and security agents. Serving as mini gods, these state humanitarian actors regulated the daily happenings in the camp, delineating who got what, when, and how much; and who left the camp, when, for how long, or for good. Undermining the authority of these actors upset the power structure in the camp and had severe repercussions for transgressors; hence, docility became a prescribed social role for IDPs. Some IDPs who chose to criticize the government or camp officials did it in a subtle way: (1) they mentioned the problems besetting IDPs in the camp; (2) they expressed gratitude for the good the government had so far done; and (3) they ended either by emphasizing that more could still be done to better their lives or by dexterously couching their request for better living conditions as a prayer to God.

The third phase of the fieldwork took place in June 2019 at the Drama Village of Ahmadu Bello University, Nigeria, and focused on a performance of the research findings, which I had turned into *Displaced*. The audience comprised students, faculty, media personnel, humanitarian workers, and the public. Then from December 12–14, 2022, I directed the first production of the play outside of Nigeria at St. Olaf College, Minnesota, with a grant from the college's Lutheran Center for Faith, Values, and Community.

Jointly set in an IDP camp in Nigeria and at the United Nations Headquarters in New York, *Displaced* follows a performance ethnographer as he relives and reframes—through omnipresent narration, choreographed flashbacks, and embodied performances—the stories of IDPs in Northeastern Nigeria. The central narration comes from the vantage point of Fatima, an 18-year-old woman who, orphaned as a child, must negotiate survival in an IDP camp with her uncle, after their near-death encounters with the bloodthirsty Boko Haram terrorists. Rather than parading her misery like a trophy or attempting suicide like her uncle—in the face of the biopolitical forces of control, exploitation, and subjugation in the camp—Fatima takes the oppressive system head-on, using theatrical reenactments to get at the truth of IDPs' existence as carceral beings.

Fatima enlists her uncle to reenact IDPs' exploitation in the camp (Ameh 13–16). The reenactment reveals IDPs' susceptibility to inducement and humanitarian actors' abuse of power. To negotiate survival in the camp, many IDPs give in to persuasion from powerful figures. This persuasion may be in the form of accepting sexual advances in a bid to secure food for oneself and one's family. Through the character of Mama Jibril, a married mother, the reenactment leads us into the world in which IDPs use sex to negotiate survival. Couched as a play-within-a-play, a dialogue between Mama Jibril and The Mask presents a picture of the negotiation process. The Mask metaphorically represents all the figures of control in the camp, including camp officials, security agents, and aid workers. In the dialogue that follows, Musa plays the role of The Mask, while Fatima embodies the character of Mama Jibril:

Musa: What do you want in my office this time, Mama Jibril?
Mama Jibril: Same thing as the last time.
Musa: My sweet sugarcane?

Mama Jibril: Food…food for me to eat...so I can feed my baby.
Musa: Then you know what to do.
Mama Jibril: I can't, this time. I gave birth only last month. I'm still sore down there.
Musa: Then I can't help you, Mama Jibril.
Mama Jibril: You know I'm not like those who say no to you when you ask them for it…I just can't now.
Musa: You're not in need. When you are, you know what to do. (16)

Preceding this dialogue, some prominent figures have come to the camp, and a camp official (The Mask) has asked IDPs to stage a performance for the entertainment of the guests. Sensing an opportunity to make their plight known to the visitors, Fatima and her uncle Musa decide to reenact IDPs' experience of sexual predation for the visitors and other IDPs to see, to the chagrin of The Mask who is seated at a corner of the stage as the performance takes place. The performance serves as an embarrassment for The Mask since it takes him unawares. Fatima and Musa's reenactment of Mama Jibril's encounter with The Mask exposes the double-facedness of The Mask and, by extension, of humanitarian actors working within the context of internal displacement in the country.

For too long, the history of IDPs has been told through the lens of the dominant group, which is made up of the government, military, media, and aid organizations (both local and international), leaving IDPs largely voiceless. Adding the voices of IDPs to the prevailing narrative of internal displacement in the Global South tells a broader and more accurate story. Beyond flipping the prevailing narrative of IDPs, it presents this historically marginalized population as active agents of change capable of making decisions about their lives. It also frames displacement as a visceral human reality as opposed to being a statistical abstraction. Displacement, for IDPs, is not about statistics but about real people floundering at the margins between hope and despair, between the never-ending present and the elusive future, and between the allure of life and the perceived imminence of death. Any reduction of displacement to mere numbers does tremendous disservice to IDPs and their experience of displacement.

Exercise

From Field to Page

Identify a social issue that piques your interest. What is a field site associated with this issue? Take a walk through this site. Use all your senses to absorb the world around you. Be attentive to the discussions, movements, sounds, smells, people, objects, anomalies, and the mundane along your way. Make a mental note of the details you notice and of your feelings. Once you have returned from your field site, take thirty minutes to write down everything you remember. Then, write a ten-minute play from your notes.

Here are some questions to ponder as you go through your notes:

1. For whom are you writing this ten-minute play?
2. What is the burning question you want to address?
3. Who are the main characters emerging from your notes?
4. How do they look?
5. What kind of clothes do they wear?
6. What do they do?
7. What objects, sounds, and visuals could you associate with these characters or the place you walked through?
8. Where are these characters situated?
9. What is your plot?
10. What do you want to emphasize in your dialogue?

Note

1 At the end of 2022, the United Nations High Commission for Refugees (UNHCR) reported 108.4 million people as forcibly displaced globally, of whom 62.5 million were IDPs, 35.3 million were refugees, and 5.4 million were asylum seekers (*Global Trends Report 2022*). For IDP data across the globe, go to the website of the Internal Displacement Monitoring Centre (IDMC): https://www.internal-displacement.org/.

Works Cited

Ameh, Elaigwu. *Displaced.* An unpublished ethnographic drama, 2019.

Internal Displacement Monitoring Centre (IDMC). "Grid 2022: Global Report on Internal Displacement." https://www.internal-displacement.org/global-report/grid2022/.

United Nations High Commissioner for Refugees. "Global Trends: Forced Displacement in 2022." https://www.unhcr.org/global-trends-report-2022.

12 Strength in Numbers

Cultivating Dramaturgical Collaboration across Disciplines

Lindsay L. Barr

In 1942, the best and brightest student engineers were plucked out of universities across the country and sent to the middle of the desert. Unbeknownst to them, in the summer of 1945, their collaboration would culminate in the invention of the atomic bomb: a technology that would irrevocably change the world and their relationship to their field of study. In 2018, a new generation of the best and brightest student storytellers tackled those young engineers' stories at Carnegie Mellon University, Pennsylvania, an institution that receives hundreds of millions of dollars in Department of Defense contract funding every year.[1]

The Way Out West by Liza Birkenmeier gives audiences a glimpse inside the secret world of Los Alamos, a top-secret laboratory atop a mesa in the New Mexico desert. A key location in the Manhattan Project, this boys' ranch school turned military installation quickly grew to house a community of 8,000. It was a restless world full of secrets, tensions, new science, and big questions. Despite (or perhaps because of) its historical setting, this world yielded an overwhelming feeling of contemporary significance. It was brimming with so much intrigue and opportunity that just one dramaturg could not hold it alone.

As a commissioned piece, *The Way Out West* was only in development for about two years before it opened as a mainstage production, meaning much of the development time overlapped with both the design and rehearsal processes. This created an exquisite crucible of collaborative dramaturgical opportunity. The overlap of all three processes meant that the script would not be solidified until technical rehearsals began. Though this is standard in many professional new play development settings, it was a new and potentially frustrating experience for most of the student actors and designers. Ensuring that development conversations were not just gate-kept to the director, dramaturg, and playwright became instrumental in keeping everyone engaged with the revision process. As the script evolved, I took care to ensure nobody felt left out of the conversation or that their discipline wasn't considered when a change was made. Additionally, because of the fluctuating script, my dramaturgical presence became even more important. Sharing the research and

DOI: 10.4324/9781032636337-15

resources I had gathered, as well as sharing insight from my conversations with the playwright, allowed the team to ground themselves in the world of the play when they couldn't yet ground themselves in the finalized text of the script.

While creating opportunities for collective acts of dramaturgy across disciplines became crucial for the piece's development, it required us to lay some groundwork and boundaries. These boundaries were important to ensure clear expectations for the cast and design team as to how much, and what kinds, of influence they could expect to see in the final product. This was still Birkenmeier's play to write, but through our collective historical research, we had the opportunity to fruitfully contribute to the development of the play, despite our expedited timeline. Early on, the playwright, director Kim Weild, and I recognized and sought to reconcile two impulses: Historical Accuracy and Emotional Connectivity. On the one hand, we wanted to stay faithful to the time and place of our setting—after all, it was chosen for a reason. On the other hand, we needed to resist the temptation to drown in the details of history. A question that helped us determine our position regarding those impulses was, "What keeps you coming back to this story?" We asked this question several times throughout the process to establish the heart of the play's inspiration and track if it changed and why. It became a helpful litmus test for future ideas and a springboard for writer's block. In this case, Birkenmeier wanted to tell a story about brilliant young people grappling with large ethical crises and discovering more about themselves along the way. The heart of the play was its relationships and characters, not its setting. Finding the balance was tricky, but we all agreed that we were telling a story, not creating a documentary. *If history fought the play, the play won*. That sentiment became a moor for the script as we dove into the sea of research.

The dual blessing/curse of working with a world-changing event was the extensive archive of declassified information available. Thanks to organizations like the Atomic Heritage Foundation and the Los Alamos Historical Society, whose missions are to preserve and make accessible atomic history, we had access to more information than we could ever use, including extensive photography, video walking tours of Los Alamos, thousands of hours of interviews, and scientific and government documentation. I encouraged the cast and designers to become a part of our research team. For the designers, this began in our initial creative meeting, where I shared my research and clarified the above ground rules. I also established that the script was going to change a lot throughout this process and communicated that the playwright was interested in their perspectives.

Because some of the most dramaturgically exciting resources I found were primary sources in the form of audio/video content, a website became the natural home for these resources instead of a static packet. The flexibility of a website also meant it could change dynamically with the still-changing script, and actors and designers could see the effects of their contributions.

One of our favorite sites became Atomic Heritage Foundation's "Voices of the Manhattan Project," a collection of interviews with people involved at all levels, from scientists to janitors to the families who had to blindly uproot their lives. These firsthand accounts were a treasure trove of character and world-building research that proved useful to everyone on the team. Working with the archives gave both actors and designers the opportunity to flex their dramaturgical muscles by learning to research the play's content broadly and filter their findings for the most emotionally resonant and therefore dramatically significant information.

Through more frequent cross-department design meetings, we created a space to dig into these archives and discuss our findings. Designers were able to use the interviews' vivid recollections of the landscape and culture to inform their early ideations. One designer introduced the Doomsday Clock by the Bulletin of Atomic Scientists: a concept that has been published since 1947 that warns the public about how close humans are to destroying the world with dangerous technologies of our own making. This became one of many shared touchpoints as we developed our own lexicon for the project; this allowed us to shift more nimbly and communicate ideas more smoothly. Through these meetings, I aimed to keep the playwright's vision and goals central despite the temptations of the many rabbit holes our research presented. I documented the ideas, questions, and provocations from the design team, filtered them, and debriefed with the director. Then, we would decide what observations might be helpful to pass on to our playwright. Introducing the idea of collective dramaturgy explicitly in my conversations with the designers helped them identify the dramaturgical work they were already doing and went a long way in establishing collaborative investment in the development process.

This became particularly useful as we conceived the second half of the play, which we called "post-bomb." The concept was that after the Trinity Test, the world of science and radioactivity had infested the very atmosphere, and the design in this section included otherworldly colors, landscapes of floating particles, and jumps through space and time. Working together, our media, scenic, and lighting designers guided the audience through the ethereal changes in space, time, and matter. By contrast, our costume and sound design grounded the audience with more familiar silhouettes and sounds they would have expected from the time period. Balancing what audiences would consider historically accurate, while leaning into some of the more fantastical visuals to emphasize the emotional stakes, kept us well within our tenets of Historical Accuracy and Emotional Connectivity. Our early collaborative research discussions facilitated crafting this second half of the play as the whole team could draw from our lexicon of research touchstones to more efficiently communicate design and narrative visions.

Once casting was finalized before summer break, I brought the actors up to speed with the research process and how we were working while the script was in flux. Cast members created personal dramaturgical materials for

Figure 12.1 Clusters of the Fuchs-inspired cards.

their characters using the resources I curated with the designers. These actor-created materials were far richer than the materials a single dramaturg could compile. The Voices of the Manhattan Project collection proved particularly useful to an actor playing a foreign-born female scientist. That actor was able to learn about real-life women who worked on the project and was able to pinpoint some useful interviews, which I screened and passed on to the playwright. Those interviews ended up cracking open a character Birkenmeier had been excited about but had been struggling to make feel whole. At each stage of the process, we presented findings like these back to the playwright, thus creating a wonderful cycle of mutual artistic generation.

Because we were all engaged in historical research from the beginning of our involvement in the show, I didn't have to spend time giving a history lesson in the first rehearsal. Instead, I got everyone on their feet, using the dramaturgical skills we had cultivated over the summer. I conducted an exercise of my own adaptation, inspired by Elinor Fuchs's "Visit to a Small Planet." After the reading and design presentations, we distributed index cards and drawing materials to the cast and designers. While reading highlights from the Fuchs sections on sight, sound, and feel, the team responded visually on their cards to each section. We then created collages and compared everyone's interpretations. Through our subsequent discussion, I documented the adjectives that came up repeatedly and seemed to resonate most. These words became very useful additions to our show lexicon (Figure 12.1).

This exercise introduced the cast to thinking about the world of the play expansively and playfully and helped them to connect with the research presentations of the design team. The cast also appreciated the chance to create something with the designers so early on in the rehearsal process. This was a great way to build a relationship between the two halves of the team and to start the generative collaborative dialogue we would need to maintain throughout the revision process. Whenever we felt a moment in the script wasn't working, the cards served as a touchpoint for us to refer to for inspiration. Thus, at each step of the process, everyone involved contributed to the play's dramaturgy, and as a result, they all felt that much closer to the world and history that our characters inhabited.

As rehearsals progressed and we neared production, the purpose and direction of the dramaturgy changed. At a certain point, the script had to freeze. Moving into tech, my primary focus became making sure everyone's dramaturgical contributions were working together. It is unusual for a new work to go from an idea to a full-budget, mainstage production in less than two years within the same organization. Given the brevity of our developmental process, the version that premiered was just that: a version. It was a step in the greater life of this work which I expect will continue to evolve.

Many dramaturgs and scholars have previously acknowledged that dramaturgical work and thinking are imperative to any theatrical or creative process and are not the sole responsibility or property of someone with the title of "capital-D" Dramaturg. Though not always recognized as such, dramaturgical research is central to creative processes including theatrical design, directing, and performance. The collective dramaturgical approach that this chapter describes emphasizes and capitalizes on the usefulness of this shared labor to the new play development process, in part, by making the unacknowledged dramaturgical labor of all members of the creative team visible and by positioning the dramaturg as facilitator of these many acts of dramaturgy. This project's collaborative approach to dramaturgy gave everyone involved a greater sense of ownership and responsibility for the piece, as well as a respect for the practice of dramaturgy. Introducing collective acts of dramaturgy, like crowdsourcing research and utilizing creative and structural exercises, kept our team connected to the world of the work even when the text itself was in flux. While this was highly useful in the original academic setting, dramaturgs and playwrights in other settings should consider adding opportunities for dramaturgical collaboration with their colleagues. Strengthening everyone's dramaturgical sensibility leads to a more communicative process and a more holistically researched product.

Exercise

A Visit to Your Planet (after Elinor Fuchs)

Goal: For all members of the team to be creatively connected to the world-building of the piece. To develop a shared vocabulary for the key feelings and senses in the world of the show.

Materials: Something to write on and many things to write with (ideally in multiple colors), selected passages from "EF's Visit to a Small Planet: Some Questions to Ask a Play."

Directions: Distribute materials and explain the scope of the exercise. Select three senses to focus on and read selections of Fuchs's questions that you feel are most relevant to your project. Allow a few minutes to respond to each prompt, collage them together, and discuss what you see. Pay attention to the vocabulary participants use, noting frequently used words. After discussing and identifying the keywords for each of the senses, document them. If space allows, keep this up in the rehearsal room with your keywords written alongside the responses. Return to and reference these as you continue to refine the play and world-build.

Lines of questioning and tips:

- "What do you see?" Start with the basics and build up the group's visual vocabulary. What are the dominant observations? Color, geometry, pattern?
- Discuss each subcategory of the essay individually. Compare the similarities and differences. Are patterns arising?
- Discuss the subcategories in relation to each other. Are there surprises? Why might the senses present differently?
- "Tell me more about that." A dramaturg's bread and butter. Encourage specificity, as this will help get to the root of the feelings.

Expansions: Feel free to take this exercise further if time allows. Asking the group to come up with movements or sounds based on the drawings may be a great way to explore the senses in an embodied way.

Note

1 "Contracts for July 1, 2020." *U.S. Department of Defense*, www.defense.gov/News/Contracts/Contract/Article/2244841/.

Works Cited

Atomic Heritage Foundation. "Voices of the Manhattan Project." *Nuclear Museum*, https://ahf.nuclearmuseum.org/voices/.

Barr, Lindsay. "*The Way Out West* Dramaturgical Website." https://lindsayturgy.wixsite.com/twowcmu.

Bulletin of the Atomic Scientists. "Doomsday Clock." *Bulletin of the Atomic Scientists*, https://thebulletin.org/doomsday-clock/.

"Contracts for July 1, 2020." *U.S. Department of Defense*, https://www.defense.gov/News/Contracts/Contract/Article/2244841/.

Fuchs, Elinor. "EF's Visit to a Small Planet: Some Questions to Ask a Play." *Theater*, vol. 34, no. 2, 2004, pp. 4–9.

13 Loops of Time

A Historicized Dramaturgy

Sam Redway

To create theatre from a historical event is to wrench it screamingly from its present to its future: our present. Creating theatre from history forges a time loop of sorts. Manfred Wekwerth, one of Bertolt Brecht's co-directors and former director of the Berliner Ensemble, explains in *Daring to Play* that "to 'historicize' something means to understand it through its historical context, so how it came about and passed away again" (37). One could interpret this as understanding the facts of the event. But this Loop of Time also involves understanding the contemporary landscape in which audiences encounter the dramatized past. This Loop of Time holds the potential for facts to become truth, turning history (in which we see others) into myth (in which we see ourselves) and making audiences feel a vertical universality ("we, the audience, have always done this"), rather than a horizontal, and more problematic, one ("we, all of humanity, do this"). It has the potential to demand audiences rethink their present by connecting to their past ("why do we still do this?"). It is *our* shared story we tell when we interpret the past. In our bodies, our voices, our choices, and our perspectives—our reasons for telling this story *now*—we reveal ourselves and our audiences. Looping our time with historical events through theatre condenses scattered moments into art, drawing links to discover and create meaning. The Loops of Time method offers a way to ensure that audiences remain connected to that meaning and see themselves reflected in the theatre.

This chapter outlines how mapping the Loop of Time between a chosen historical event and our contemporary lives informed the co-created retelling of the Macclesfield Potato Riot of 1812 with 60 Macclesfield residents of all ages in 2017. Macclesfield is a postindustrial market town in Cheshire, UK. While the industrial past of Macclesfield is evident in the architecture (and its nickname "Silktown"), an ailing high street and rising unemployment indicated its modern struggles at the time. In 2004, *The Times* newspaper called Macclesfield the least cultured town in the UK, causing a spike in cultural activity, including the Barnaby Festival, Treacle Market, and Heritage Centres. Free and open to the public, this reenactment of a formative but mostly forgotten moment in the town's history was a first. I was commissioned by

DOI: 10.4324/9781032636337-16

Community Arts Space Macclesfield (CASM) to support the community's dramatization of this riot as a promenade performance, based on the narrative of the original riot documented in an article in the *Chester Courant*'s April 21, 1812 issue. To support participants in taking theatrical command of the historical event, I needed to uncover why to retell this story now. With 60 community members and inconsistent attendance, this project could lack focus and, consequently, lack quality, and so negatively impact the town's arts engagement long-term. A shared process of clarifying the loop between 1812 and 2017 created an established reference document for all participants, improving focus and allowing participants and audiences to better feel the contemporary resonances of history and more readily recognize the value of the retelling. Three broad stages emerged: Understanding the Event, Connections, and Creation. There is some linearity to this, but as with all creative processes, expect some circles in practice. This method can be used to clarify process and outcome at all stages of work, from concept to production.

Stage One—Understanding the Event

To create site-specific theatre of this reenactment and wrench this historic riot into our present, we needed to go beyond the facts into the mythic, political, and historical resonances in the story: how it felt and what it meant. To paraphrase political economist Keir Milburn, how did the riot of 1812 disrupt the way that Macclesfield makes sense of itself (18)? In 1812, as many communities across industrial UK were struggling with the rising costs of living and diminishing employment opportunities, riots were an increasingly common occurrence, generating various dissident groups including the mill-breaking Cropper Lads of Yorkshire and Ned Ludd and his Luddites. The Macclesfield riot itself was an anti-industrialist, Luddite rebellion (their mythical namesake, Ned Ludd, himself may have participated) against the rising cost of potatoes concurrent with the falling wages of laborers. The riot was a disruptor of the story that industrialization at all costs was unquestionably good. To support the participants in developing their artistic, historicized retelling, I worked to uncover the original riot's connections to the participants' shared story as a town with rising unemployment in 2017. If we understood the lead-up and impact of the riot, seen through the lens of our 2017 context, could we identify a shared story to disrupt?

The ensemble varied from 20 to 60 members of the Macclesfield community who had signed up as CASM regulars or through taster workshops offered earlier in the process. Our project timeline was tight: one session a week for eight weeks. A codification of process was essential to enable thematic and creative handover across the fluid attendance. Inspired by the work of dramaturg Nina Steiger (National Theatre, UK), I developed an exercise that would allow us to systematize the time loops we wanted to dramatize. Where Steiger's method prompts artists to consider the scales of impact of an

Table 13.1 An abbreviated version of time loop chart one

Past	*Present: April 13, 1812*	*Future*
• Preindustrial Britain wages fixed to the price of food • Circa 1700: Industrial Revolution begins • Rising unemployment vs. rising wealth of mill owners • 1799: Combination Acts signed, banning collective bargaining • 1811: first large-scale Luddite riot in Arnold, Nottingham (machinery broken)	• Market day, workers unable to afford potatoes on the current wage • Townsfolk throw potatoes to protest their price • Riot breaks out • Political speeches: Riot Act is read and the riot is put down by the cavalry	• 1812: Prime Minister assassinated • 1813: 14 Luddites hanged in Manchester • 1824: Combination Acts repealed • Fear of minimum wage becoming maximum • Gradual decline of collective power • Self-service checkouts

Table 13.2 An abbreviated version of time loop chart two

Past	*Present: 2017*	*Future*
• The riot of 1812 • 1960–1990: Closure of mines and selling off of public assets • Mass protests ignored • Margaret Thatcher "breaking" the unions • 2016: Member of Parliament murdered	• Rising unemployment/ insecure employment • Self-service checkouts • Rising cost of living • Democratic crisis • Industry stifling action on climate change	?

event across time, my exercise asks participants to compare the arcs of two distinct time periods in order to reveal latent similarities or connections.[1] To understand this event, I asked participants to fill out two charts, each using a three-stage timeline (Past, Present, Future). Chart one takes the present to be the present of the historical event dramatized (1812). Chart two takes the present to be the theatre-makers' present (2017). In comparing these charts, we were able to visualize the time loops and shared contours between timelines. The first chart (contracted for illustrative purposes) ended up something like Table 13.1, while the second chart resembled Table 13.2.

What emerged was an understanding that while the 1812 riot appeared at first to be a moment of public empowerment and progress in the short-term, it arguably provoked a long-term rejection of the rioters' attempted disruption of the prevailing story. The participants started to feel like they were telling a tragedy and that the riot was functioning as an origin story prefiguring the 2017 problems. For example, the Luddite riots pushing back against the mechanization of the workforce connected deeply to the participants' protests against the increasing prevalence of self-service checkouts in the local area. One participant even asked, "Whose story are we telling: ours in 2017 or the original rioters'?"

Completing this task with a community theatre group with fluid attendance and a primary ethos toward empowerment and creative ownership meant my dramaturgical role became facilitative. Endowing all gathered responses with equal legitimacy without imposing curatorial input would result in a cumbersome amount of information and lack of clarity in the thematic drive. But to curate the community's responses alone would be to set myself up as an arbiter of their experiences rather than a facilitator of the performance-making process. To maintain democratic empowerment within the process of interpretation, I opted to narrow down the generated content by degrees of connection and consent. First, if there were any repeats or near-synonyms, the group elected which iteration would be kept. Next, if a concept was caught within another, the group would acknowledge one as an umbrella to the other. For example, "Democratic Crisis" holds several ideas (disproportionate representation, distrust in politicians, voter despair), enabling all participants who raised the contributing ideas to be valued through the creative process without risking a dilution of focus. But the key method to narrow down and find creative perspective was to look for connections between 1812 and the participants' thoughts, feelings, and concerns in 2017.

Stage Two—Connections

We discovered that there were three categories of connection through this process:

Event Connection

An event in this context is simply something that changes the people around it. Event Connections occur when the contours of a given event remain consistent across time regardless of the specifics. This could be either a moment (e.g., a mass protest) or a process (e.g., mechanization of labor). They may not fit in the same time bracket (past, present, future), but creating a picture of Event Connections reveals shared attitudes between the historical event and now (e.g., the murder of politicians in both timelines points to a similarity of climate).

Thematic Connection

Thematic Connections are linked to Event Connections but are less tangible and more symbolic. They reveal similarities in cultural attitudes or philosophical positions, which underpin events (e.g., democratic crisis). Examination of Thematic Connections opens up conversations around allegory, metaphor, changing cultural interpretations of events, and participants' reasons for representing them. When the 1812 riot reenactors throw potatoes to protest the overpricing of essential goods, would it be more effective for our audiences to see something else thrown? What would be the contemporary equivalent? We discussed this, but decided that as this reenactment was of the "Potato Riot," potatoes should remain the protest prop.

Timeline Connection

With an understanding of the Event and Thematic Connections between 1812 and 2017, I asked participants to discuss whether we, in 2017, were building to a riot or were living in the political/economic consequences of one. This yielded a unanimous response that, given the similarity between the political factors at play in 1812 and 2017, we were building to one. Our reenactment could feel like a natural progression, rather than a diversion, from our social context. We could all imagine a riot taking place in the not-too-distant future. The group decided they wanted to use this reenactment to connect with their audiences' real-world discontent, to focus the audience on what they might riot for, and to gather a crowd in demonstration for a better future.

So far, we had generated a shared historicized understanding of the riot of 1812 and of how our retelling in 2017 connected with the themes and events of 1812. This understanding of the connections generated many answers to why the reenactors wanted to retell the riot now: each participant had their own reasons to riot. Engaging with these loops of time had delivered a compass to discovery: a written, physical reminder of our shared intention pinned up on the wall. This document could be referred back to at any point in the rehearsal to set the course of travel, whether or not participants had attended before. The group wanted their riot to foment subversive political activism around a diverse set of issues for Macclesfield now. They wanted to create a disruptor of the story Macclesfield was telling of itself and wanted audience members to become the riot itself. They hoped audiences would take space and air their concerns, anxieties, and anger. While the group's creative and political intentions would be clear, there had to be space for each audience member to riot on their own behalf. Much like in a real riot, there would be a single trigger point, but individuals' reasons would be as plural as the individuals present and would be drawn from the political and economic realities of 1812 and of 2017.

Stage Three—Creation

It was important to maintain our shared creative intentions as a constant reference point while creating and rehearsing with an ever-changing participant pool. We couldn't change the major events of the 1812 riot, but the words would be semi-improvised and the scenic focus could draw from 2017 or 1812. When reenactors confronted employers about diminishing opportunities, the argument would sometimes focus around Tesco supermarkets in 2017 and sometimes around the innovations in loom technology in 1812. The actors all knew the game and would play it together. The performance's sense of character would be derived from the form and energy of a riot: occasionally, one person (Ned Ludd, the yeoman, the local landlord) would draw sharp focus for a time before disappearing, but ultimately, the crowd became the protagonist in the narrative, trying to disrupt and shift the passage of history. The Loop of Time became especially vibrant as the events of 1812 were happening in the very spots where they happened originally. Drawing focus to the loop in time, the contemporary resonance brought the devisers' intentions together and drew audiences' concerns to the fore to develop a dramaturgy of their own. Agitators handing papier-mâché potatoes out for audience members to throw, offering soap boxes to audience members to articulate their reasons for rioting, giving speeches themselves, and a live cavalry halting the march of the audience, all contributed to the performance generating the riot afresh in a Loop of Time. This dramaturgy took a unique "both-times" feel as moments would slip from one to the other, and the audience played along. One audience member took to a box to protest the planned sale of a local peat bog (Danes Moss) to developers; another challenged us to refuse to work for tuppence-a-week. Whether this Loop of Time provoked any long-term shift in perspective is impossible to tell. But, for a moment, it certainly felt like Macclesfield was collectively asking, "Why do we *still* allow industrial progress to be at the cost of our living?"

Exercise

Try uncovering the Loop of Time in your adaptation of a historical event:

- Individually, fill out the "past, present, future" chart with everything you know about the historical event you are adapting for performance, using the present of the event.
- Create a "past, present, future" chart using your contemporary moment as the present.
- If working in a group, compare your filled-out charts and discuss any divergences or differences in interpretation you have in your charts.

Notes

1 I originally encountered Steiger's work through an interview on the Dramaturg's Network referenced here: https://www.dramaturgy.co.uk/single-post/2016/02/18/Interview-with-Dramaturg-Nina-Steiger. The full text of the interview is,

unfortunately, no longer available online. I then encountered her work, again, through a workshop with Bryony Kimmings cited below.

Works Cited

Milburn, Keir. *Generation Left*. Polity Press, 2020.

Steiger, Nina. *Digging Through the Darkness: Finding the Bones of Your Best Stories. Bryony Kimmings Workshops*, 23 July 2020. https://www.bryonykimmings.com/education.html.

Wekwerth, Manfred. *Daring to Play: A Brecht Companion*, edited by Anthony Hozier. Routledge, 2011.

Part III

Dramaturgy and/as Public History

Connecting with Broader Publics

14 Hands-On History

Engaging Historical Thinking through Dramaturgy

Elysia Segal

Located within a historic, former Naval aircraft carrier in New York City, the Intrepid Museum promotes the awareness and understanding of history, science, and service through its collections, exhibitions, and programming (Intrepid Museum). With an ever-present eye toward STEAM (science, technology, engineering, arts, and math) education and drawing inspiration from its vast collection of artifacts, the museum recently concluded its successful, five-year performance outreach residency, *Crossing the Line: Bringing History to Life with Teens*, which utilized the dramaturgical process of creating primary source-based performances as an adaptable teaching tool for use in schools and communities. This program guided students through the interdisciplinary theory and practice of dramatic composition to connect historical figures and events to their lives and experiences. By embracing the inherent storytelling found within history and interpreting their discoveries through a variety of performance styles, students ultimately created and presented their own history-inspired pieces. As a result, they developed deeper historical understanding, flexed their problem-solving and critical thinking skills, cultivated their social-emotional growth, and expressed their creativity in a fun and engaging way.

Program Background

The program was born out of the concept of using museum theatre and historical interpretation to teach content and inspire a deeper appreciation of history.[1] The museum has previously presented a variety of public performances of this nature, including a recreation of a World War II-era radio show and a first-person interpretation of a teenage aviatrix from the 1920s. Embracing this format but taking its application a step further, the goal of *Crossing the Line* was to encourage the use of a more dramaturgical approach to interpreting the past to encourage students to think outside of the box: to look deeper into the relationships and situations that bring history to life and stir an emotional connection. The program encouraged greater historical understanding

DOI: 10.4324/9781032636337-18

by providing an adaptable approach to the *creation* process, promoting more thorough historical research skills and analysis imbued with an empathetic understanding of history perfectly suited for use by others in educational settings.

The title of the program, *Crossing the Line*, came from a time-honored Naval tradition, the "Line Crossing Ceremony," that began about four hundred years ago and continues onboard Naval ships today. Since the dawn of seafaring, sailors would pray to Neptune, the God of the Sea, to ask for protection. The Line Crossing Ceremony celebrates a sailor's symbolic transformation from a slimy "Pollywog," one who has never crossed the "line" of the Equator, to a trusty "Shellback," who has become part of a fellowship of seasoned sailors. It allows them to honor nautical tradition, to test their seaworthiness, and to mark a milestone with elaborate costumes, talent shows, and memorable bonding experiences.

The name was a perfect nod to Naval history, and ultimately, the students did end up "proving themselves" through their hard work, research, writing, and creativity. They began as Pollywogs with varying degrees of research experience and knowledge about primary sources or historical events, and throughout the program, they learned creative ways to interpret history. By the end, they became seasoned Shellbacks, armed with knowledge, research skills, and a creative piece to present to their peers.

Program Overview and Structure

Across ten sessions, students explored primary source materials from the museum's collection that related to their class's chosen topic of World War II, the Space Race, or the Vietnam War. They also studied dramaturgical techniques and presentation styles and formats, before ultimately creating their original performances, which were presented for friends and family.

Notably, the program's ten-session format could be tailored around a given site's schedule, with each session's content scaled to fill a class length from 45 minutes to two hours. The sessions were conducted over two weeks to three months, depending on the site's schedule. This flexibility proved very helpful for host teachers who oversaw differing class lengths or afterschool programs throughout the year.

The first day of the program consisted of a museum site visit, inclusive of a tour focused on the selected program theme and a guest speaker or hands-on demonstration. This was followed by four more days (Days 2–5) of content and an exploration of performance styles delivered by a museum teaching artist at the host site. During this first half of the program, each session began with a short writing prompt to encourage students to think more critically about what they had been learning and to connect the content to their own lived experiences, strengthening personal connections and developing their empathy skills (see Table 14.1). Students also learned techniques in concept

Table 14.1 Sample writing prompts

Daily Writing Prompts	*Artist Statement Guiding Questions*
• **Day 2**—What experience from your visit to the museum stood out to you the most? Why? (Alternatively: What would you like to know more about? Why?) • **Day 3**—What themes have you found in the readings? Write about a time when one of these themes appeared in your own life. • **Day 4**—What are different ways you can tell a story? How might you convey different moods (e.g., happy, sad, scared, etc.) without words? • **Day 5**—Over the past few lessons, what moods or emotions have the readings/images made you feel?	• What topics and/or themes does your piece reflect? Why did you choose to explore them? • What do you hope to learn, share, or expose by exploring these topics? • Are there any similarities between your topic and issues being faced by people today? • What performance style have you chosen and why did you choose it? • Discuss your process of researching and creating your performance. • What challenges did you encounter while creating your performance? How did you overcome them? • What sources and inspiration contributed to your work? • What have you learned since writing this piece? • How do you hope your performance informs or impacts your audience?

mapping and organizing ideas while performing close investigations of primary source materials strategically paired with each day's learning goals. Students interpreted these sources and identified themes that could be referred to later while creating their performances.

More specifically, Day 2 focused on teaching these foundational skills through the examination of written primary sources with an emphasis on descriptive language and conveying emotion through words. Then, during Day 3, students studied the physicality displayed in photographs and noted elements such as facial expressions and body language before creating physical tableaus. They also explored the development of unique characters through guided movement exercises. Day 4 introduced alternative ways to tell a story, including analysis of historical song lyrics (for instance, David Bowie's "Space Oddity"), soundscapes, and Foley art, complete with in-class demonstrations and hands-on experimentation. Finally, Day 5 investigated the pros and cons of incomplete information. Students were encouraged to be discerning in their research while also acknowledging that historical and science fiction can be an exciting springboard for creativity. For instance, in the case of the Space Race topic, we scientifically debunked several Moon landing conspiracy theories to highlight how easily misinformation and bias can lead researchers offtrack, but also shared a few well-documented yet still unexplained astronaut experiences to allow students to brainstorm their own creative theories.

On Day 6, students were asked to select one of the many themes that they had identified from the materials as a central theme for their final presentation. Acknowledging that some students might feel performance anxiety, the final project prompt was always left open-ended, allowing students to explore new techniques or embrace familiar, preexisting passions. The concept of an Artist Statement was then introduced alongside a worksheet with guiding questions that helped them to start, focus, and refine their work, as well as track their progress along the way (see Table 14.1 and "*Evaluation Methods*" for more on the Artist Statement). This day also featured the presentation of artistic samples about the topic such as music videos, puppetry, dance, and spoken word poetry to provide further inspiration.

The remainder of the program (Days 7–10) consisted of student research and writing for their final performances, either individually or in small groups. The teaching artist helped to guide students through any challenges that arose; offered additional resources or inspiration where necessary; provided constructive feedback on their work; sourced any costumes, props, or sets that the students requested; and aided them throughout the rehearsal process. The students' final performances were then presented either at their site or back at the museum on the final day.

Ultimately, student performance modes included theatre and performance art, puppetry, inspirational speeches, letters and journal entries, films, animation, radio drama, a video blog, poetry, music, dance, and live interpretation of original artwork. Additionally, with the worldwide pivot to online programming during the COVID-19 pandemic, students became increasingly interested in presentation techniques that also flexed their use of digital dramaturgy through the incorporation of video filters, special effects, artistic title slides, or underscored music. These integrations suggested that students were giving even more critical thought to the development, delivery, and presentation aspects of their finished projects—further applying their dramaturgical thinking to shape their works on a broader scale.

But the creativity didn't stop there—some students even came up with their own unique interpretations and "spins" on history. For instance, one pandemic-era student shared that she aspired to become a culinary chemist when she grew up, and she also really loved baking shows. With some guidance, she was able to infuse the Space Race into a baking show format that featured her making Gemini constellation cookies (little stars connected by toothpicks) and a Moon landing cake with gray regolith frosting and craters, all while weaving in historical context throughout her show.

Another performance featured a "dance-off" between students dressed in shirts representing the United States and the Soviet Union—a movement-based interpretation of the "Space Race" rivalry between these two countries. Yet another group wrote a play exploring what might have happened if American astronaut Neil Armstrong and Soviet cosmonaut Valentina Tereshkova, the first woman in space, had worked together and had become the first two people to land on the Moon, together. Others staged an original puppet show featuring a time-traveling photo booth that put the main characters (from present-day) into the roles of the original Apollo 11 astronauts. A number of performances also highlighted the underrepresented achievements of women during the Space Race, including "hidden figure" Katherine Johnson, a NASA (National Aeronautics and Space Administration) mathematician of orbital mechanics, and the Mercury 13, the first women to undergo astronaut testing during the early days of the space program.

Evaluation Methods

The primary goals outlined for *Crossing the Line* were threefold:

1. To provide rich, engaging humanities-based experiences to underserved youth throughout the New York City (NYC) area in order to increase students' academic motivation, historical knowledge, and use and analysis of primary and secondary sources
2. To use performance and the creation thereof as a means of developing historical understanding, increasing problem-solving skills, and cultivating social-emotional growth
3. To deepen the museum's longstanding relationships with a number of partner sites through youth involvement and the attendance of the students' friends, family, and other community members during final performances

The residency's evaluative methods thus measured performance indicators closely aligned to these program goals (see Table 14.2). In addition to in-class observations and evaluation of their final projects, students also completed self-evaluative, qualitative performance indicator surveys using a five-point Likert scale to monitor their growth from the beginning to the end of the program. After the completion of each cohort, students reported considerable increases in confidence, competence, and motivation compared with their self-reported levels of knowledge and comfort at the beginning of the program. They also reported an increase in the ability to find connections between themselves and historical people or events and the belief that art was a good way to learn about history.

Furthermore, the student-created Artist Statements also encouraged targeted reflection on their artistic process and growth throughout the residency. Prompts included why they chose to explore the specific topics and themes of their performance piece, a discussion of their creative process including challenges they encountered and how they overcame them, citing which sources provided inspiration for their work, and describing how they hoped their performance would be received by the audience, both cognitively and emotionally.

Throughout the *Crossing the Line* program, nearly three hundred students connected historical figures and events to their own lives and experiences,

Table 14.2 Program goals and evaluative evidence

Goals *As a result of this program, students will be able to...*	**Evidence** *To show proficiency in this area, students will produce...*
Develop a deeper understanding of a historical event, including connections to a broader context.	• Student work products are factual and include reference to a wider historical context • Pre- and post-group concept maps
Identify personal challenges and strategies used to overcome obstacles during the creation of a performance piece.	• Student reflections included in their Artist Statements
Make personal connections to historical events.	• Performance • Journal Entries • Artist Statement
Understand how to analyze and interpret primary and secondary sources (reliability and limitations, purpose and perspective) in order to build a strong thesis.	• Students provide source-based evidence for their interpretive choices in their Artist Statement • Student work products show an interpretive point of view
Engage others with history through writing and performance	• Audience tracking

forging a link between the past and the present. The results demonstrated that a dramaturgical approach toward the creation of a historical performance can have a profound impact on fostering academic skills and encouraging social-emotional growth while exposing the next generation to the uniquely creative field of historical interpretation.

Exercise

Select a primary source and encourage students to use dramaturgical skills to analyze the document. Working broadly at first, have them consider:

- What type of document is it?
- What historical event does it describe or relate to?
- Does it fit with what they already know about the topic?

Next, have students dig deeper by exploring the social, political, or historical context of the document, as well as any use of storytelling or descriptive and figurative language.

- How does the way it was written make them feel? Why?
- What universal themes can they find in the writing?
- Have they ever felt any of those themes in their own life?

Have students consider the perspective of the author, then write and perform their own short monologues describing a personal experience that relates to a theme found in the document.

Note

1 For scholarship that demonstrates the efficacy of such programs, see (among others) Catherine Hughes, Tessa Bridal, Anthony Jackson, and Jenny Kidd's work on the subject.

Works Cited

Bridal, Tessa. *Exploring Museum Theatre*. Altamira Press, 2004.

Hughes, Catherine. *Museum Theatre: Communicating with Visitors through Drama*. Heinemann, 1998.

"Intrepid Museum – About Us." *Intrepid Museum*, 2024, https://intrepidmuseum.org/about-us.

Jackson, Anthony, and Jenny Kidd, eds. *Performing Heritage: Research, Practice and Innovation in Museum Theatre and Live Interpretation*. Manchester University Press, 2012.

Kidd, Jenny. "Filling the Gaps? Interpreting Museum Collections through Performance." *Journal of Museum Ethnography*, vol. 19, March 2007, pp. 57–69.

15 Applying Brecht's Anti-Spectacular Approach to Staging Fascism

Ilinca Tamara Todoruț

In 2024, at a time of global climate crisis, widening wealth gaps, financial-sector deregulation, and concomitant depressions, media-fueled right-wing discourses are, again, gaining traction, inviting comparisons to the upheavals of the previous century. Written between 1938 and 1939, on the footsteps of the Great Depression and before the magnitude of fascist destruction reached its peak in the twentieth century, Bertolt Brecht's *Fear and Misery of the Third Reich* (*Furcht Und Elend Des Dritten Reiches*) trades in slowly accruing mundane acts of injustice. Brecht referred to it as "a documentary play" about "behavioral patterns" ("Further Note" 327). The play shows a sliding toward catastrophe as ordinary people try to carry on their normal lives by adjusting to increasingly violent realities. *Fear and Misery* illustrates anti-spectacular dramaturgical approaches, which are staging and narrative techniques that avoid the sensational in order to show that violence rabidly erupts in wars and genocides, but also lives ingrained in the fabric of our daily existence. The approaches include anti-dramatic narratives dispensing of hero-villain polarities, and historical frameworks scaled down to the quotidian that grant agency to individuals, while also recognizing large-scale systemic forces. Such dramaturgical strategies suit performance projects aiming to call for collective action against forces that perpetuate injustices, crimes, and human rights violations. I will illustrate their tactical application in a 2021 high school production on teenage anxiety called *Success*.

The Anti-Dramatic

In 1916, literary theorist György Lukács argued in *Theory of the Novel* that twentieth-century history, due to its nebula of socioeconomic processes and political actors, can only be properly treated by the novel's richer narrative resources and not by the theatre's reductionist dramaturgy of limited temporal and spatial frames and few actants. One world war later, Brecht ventured to put on stage the historical mess of the Nazi rise to power over the course of the 1930s. In *Fear and Misery*, Brecht employed a history-from-below

DOI: 10.4324/9781032636337-19

approach that dissected the growing right-wing extremism among various strata of the populace. The play unfurls in short, pugnacious vignettes written while in exile, drawn from a mix of newspaper clippings, personal and hearsay experiences, and fictionalized accounts. Scenes jump in time and space, scroll through characters, and play with a range of tones from comedic and absurdist to tragic and sentimental. A middle-class couple listens to the authorities coming for a neighbor they reported for the illegal activity of listening to foreign broadcasts. In a well-to-do kitchen, domestic employees of opposite political affinities tensely discuss matters of public policy, including abortion. A judge is swayed by political pressures to acquit the perpetrators of violent attacks. Doctors and scientists avoid discussing politics at all costs, but opportunistically exorcise "tainted" elements from their communities (here, Einstein, a Jew). A couple fears their child will report them to the authorities because they expressed critical views. Farmers feed their pigs properly, despite official rationing regulations. If high-ranking decision-makers appear in the scenes, they do so only as disembodied voices blaring from a radio, such as Hitler's spreading misinformation through the media.

This disparate collection of "playlets" or "short sketches" were written in simple language and unintimidating realistic style with discernible characters and mini-narratives with amateur theatre-makers and affordable production costs in mind (Kuhn and Willet xii–xiii). From the total of 30 scenes printed in the Methuen Drama volume, theatre groups can select to present any number in any order, although most productions and printed versions of the texts choose to line them up in chronological order of instances portrayed from 1933 to 1938. Tom Kuhn and John Willett unequivocally write that "there is no trace of any structural scheme for this work" (346). If dramaturgy is structure, meaning a "purposeful arrangement of events" (2) to use Magda Romanska's clear definition of a central tenet of dramatic theory, then Brecht conceived *Fear and Misery* as anarchically anti-dramatic. As if the first exercise for members of a populace scared into submission could be the dramaturgical process of choice-making in constructing a narrative. Brecht offers a figurative set of training wheels in the process of unlearning inherited structures and inventing new ones.

Lukács praised *Fear and Misery* for its naturalism. Brecht retorted with jibes at a Lukács who didn't understand the theatre, highlighting the principle of montage at the dramaturgical heart of a distinctly anti-dramatic play that discards Aristotelian ideas of character, plot, and unified action, time, and space for a popular mode of theatricality characterized by episodic, fast, pared-down sketches in mixed register. "It is just a table of gests," wrote Brecht, a gallery view or a panorama of what people do under nationalist, racist, repressive leadership (Kuhn and Willett xxi). For Brecht, the anti-dramatic approach translates to an embrace of popular performance modes reminiscent of the Weimar variety shows where Bavarian artists like comedian Karl

Valentin entertained audiences in Munich's beerhalls and cabarets. Brecht never insulted the public's intelligence by suggesting that it can best be served by facile plots, mass-produced structures, and black-and-white moralizing. *Fear and Misery* is simple in design, but not simplistic.

The Anti-Historiographical

Fear and Misery is designed on a modest scale dramaturgically (as playlets), aesthetically (as unglamorously realistic), artistically (as low-budget friendly), politically (as a popular, non-elitist form inviting amateur performances), and conceptually (as an unspectacular, low-brow version of historical events). These de-dramatization strategies align with a particular treatment of historical narrative.

Walter Benjamin, Brecht's collaborator, criticized historicism for its dramatic, plot-like, causal, and teleological arrangement of events. Benjamin points out that historiography shares with the dramatic the taste for the sensational and the monumental. Such tastes glorify the pile of human squabbles into a grand, Hegelian, well-structured narrative of historical acts. Instead of conceiving of history as a "sequence of events like the beads of the rosary," Benjamin encourages a panoramic, all-at-once grasping of "the constellation" of occurrences, of the plethora of manifestations, positions, and missed opportunities (263). For Brecht and Benjamin alike, representing history on stage without theatricalizing it meant a portrayal of the past that deflates its causal inevitability and suggests that our present always remains open to change.

Benjamin's conception of historical investigation as the practice of rag-picking through the trash heap of discarded options manifests in *Fear and Misery*'s leveling treatment of historical actors and events, where a servant and a doctor receive equal stage time. In *Fear and Misery*, Brecht becomes Benjamin's idea of "a chronicler who recites events without distinguishing between major and minor ones" since every occurrence stands in, monad-like, for the whole (254). Every event registers—in its petty violence or droplets of courage and integrity—the larger context of systemic oppression and resistance. Every moment can be cited as evidence for hegemony's continued imposition on the fabric of existence and an undefeated resistance to its concrete and discursive rule.

Neither the extent of violence nor the resistance to it should be minimized; nor should one be prioritized over the other. Ignoring past and present resistance decimates hope and recounts history from the warped perspective of the victors. Minimizing the depths of violence leads to the ahistorical, unphilosophical "amazement that the things we are experiencing are 'still' possible in the twentieth century" (Benjamin 257). And the twenty-first century.

Twenty-First-Century Applications

I will show the relevance of anti-spectacular approaches to staging history for a tenth-grade high school production on teenage anxiety called *Success*, put on in 2021 for an audience of fellow students and staff members as part of a Theatre course I was teaching at United World College Changshu China. The economic boom initiated in the 1980s by Deng Xiaoping came hand in hand with an environment of intense competition starting from the school benches. As in many other countries today, students' mental and physical health as well as their social development are impacted by pervading worries related to their future, constant academic and peer pressure, and fraught romantic, collegial, or filial relationships. Referred to in English as "involution," the Chinese term for the social phenomena brought on by the effects of competition is *nèijuǎn* [内卷], a compound word that describes the action of rolling inward or folding inside oneself. After years of teaching at the school, I attempted to give voice to some of the students' feelings. I wrote eight original scenes and adapted two other ones, one from Karen Tei Yamashita's short story collection *Sensei and Sensibility* and the other from a David Yoon novel called *Frankly in Love*, both of which treat the theme of high academic expectations that "Tiger" parents have of their children.

Consisting of ten scenes in total and 34 characters for that many student roles, the show lays out in direct language and simple actions a constellation of daily occurrences gravitating around large-scale historical and political realities. It highlights the mistreatment inflicted upon young people by the corporatized culture of work and education, aiming to suggest, like *Fear and Misery*, that what may seem small prefigures grave future dangers. One kid tries to articulate their repressed fears and desires to a parent, and vice versa; another literally runs through the full day of a micromanaged, packed schedule; another two try to figure out what kind of inter-student physical contact their boarding school's inconclusive student handbook allows. Realistic scenes alternate with more stylized ones, where students play psychomachia-like conflicting inner voices or take on the role of an anthropomorphized timetable. Similarly, heavier dramatic scenes mingle with comedic ones driven by the delusions of a superhero called Superstudent.

As the playwright, I employed strategies of de-dramatization to fracture conventional notions of plot in favor of minute occurrences that require swift transitions and thus cannot accommodate elaborate sets and costumes. We staged the show in an outdoor amphitheater, a location intentionally open to accidental spectators. Freed from the labor of set design and construction, the performers dedicated more time to staging and coordinating actions in a quick-moving variety show that compensated for the lack of visual spectacle or impressive tech with the attention-grabbing swiftness of constantly changing characters, situations, environments, and moods.

I wrote *Success* to accommodate the students' wide range of experience with live performance and starkly different levels of aptitude with the English language. In its (dramatically and historically) unspectacularized and modest form, the show welcomed amateur performers, some of whom had never acted before. The many different types of characters necessitating varying degrees of physical and vocal expression gave students choice in who to perform, in what style, and with how many lines, allowing them to pick roles that suited their tastes, abilities, and comfort level. As a dramaturg, I worked to engage a diversity of students and empower them each as valued and essential contributors. I employed the dramaturgy of a segmented narrative with many characters as an opportunity to facilitate nonhierarchical working methods, where students took on responsibility for small and manageable parts of the final product. As a first performance at the start of the year in a new school (housing students grades ten to twelve only), the production built the foundation for fruitful collaborations. It also inspired the students to trust in their own powers and articulate their points of view. For the next unit, all students wrote original scenes, and they voted on which ones to subsequently stage.

The experience of staging *Success* collaboratively with my students revealed in practice Brecht's complex understanding of the interplay between content, form, and working methods, and the necessity of their interrelation in a project aiming to make a mark within a local community. The sprawling of varied occurrences within the dramaturgy of the play text encouraged students to recognize some of their own attitudes shared by dramatized figures. *Success* sketches out the imprints of big sociohistorical and economic mechanisms upon the intimate fabrics of daily life, highlighting at the same time the gests of compliance and of refusal. The scenes avoid historiographical narratives of main characters and powerful figures directing the course of events. As a result, they undercut the political illusion that only the powerful can initiate change. What was once experienced as private, singular, and inconsequential is revealed to be collective, shared, and the very locus of a potential revolution—without privatizing the burden of change to the individual level.

Exercise

The themes broached by politicized community performances—including racism, *nèijuǎn*, and climate catastrophe—are invariably heavy and bleak. The typical first impulse is to honor the import of the subject with a ponderous approach that often veers into the sensational and the sentimental. Such approaches risk artistic clichés and inefficiency because the complexity of the issue overwhelms participants who then treat it in abstract and generalized terms that dim the relevance to their lived realities. So during rehearsals, exercises should aim to ground the issues into palpable aspects of participants' own lives.

A useful prompt asks participants to bring in physical objects from their daily life that relate to the given theme. These objects act as anchors to their realities and should be incorporated in improvisations and even in the final show. For *Success*, students brought heavy textbooks, alarm clocks, and junk food. If, for example, the theme is climate change, participants may be tasked to bring a physical thing that only exists in their neighborhood because of climate change (if it's a living being, they should take a picture instead). Then, invite participants to improvise a scene based on one, two, or all of their objects. Individuals may choose to share their object's story or not. Alternatively, participants randomly swap objects, and at first, they sit privately with the new object in their charge to "hear" its story by interacting with it sensuously. Then, they can share the object's story. Lastly, the group stages and acts out each story.

Works Cited

Benjamin, Walter. "Theses on the Philosophy of History." *Illuminations: Essays and Reflections*, edited by Hannah Arendt. Translated by Harry Zohn. Schocken Books, 2007, pp. 253–64.

Brecht, Bertolt. "Fear and Misery of the Third Reich." *Brecht Collected Plays: Four*, edited by Tom Kuhn and John Willett. Collaborator M. Steffin. Translated by John Willett. Methuen Drama, 2001, pp. 115–206.

Brecht, Bertolt. "Further Note." *Brecht Collected Plays: Four*, edited by Tom Kuhn and John Willett. Methuen Drama, 2001, p. 327.

Kuhn, Tom and John Willett. "Editorial Notes." *Brecht Collected Plays: Four*, edited by Tom Kuhn and John Willett. Methuen Drama, 2001, pp. 346–54.

Kuhn, Tom and John Willett. "Introduction." *Brecht Collected Plays: Four*, edited by Tom Kuhn and John Willett. Methuen Drama, 2001, pp. vii–xxix.

Romanska, Magda. "Introduction." *The Routledge Companion to Dramaturgy*, edited by Magda Romanska. Routledge, 2015, pp. 1–15.

Yamashita, Karen Tei. "Monterey Park." *Sensei and Sensibility*. Coffee House Press, 2020, pp. 133–41.

Yoon, David. *Frankly in Love*. Putnam, 2019.

16 "Beyond Land Acknowledgement"

Rendering Central Illinois History along the Potawatomi Trail of Death

Nicole Anderson Cobb

Allerton Park & Retreat Center is a renowned public park and research center for wildlife donated to the University of Illinois, Urbana-Champaign (UIUC) from artist and philanthropist Robert Allerton in 1946.[1] Consequently, Allerton, located in Monticello, Illinois, has been designated one of the Seven Wonders of Illinois and is listed on the National Register of Historic Places (Holtz 8). Yet, there is another story: the pre-Allerton story of the land, a First Nation story that predates Eastern elite Samuel Allerton purchasing the 12,000 acres that would include the Allerton estate in 1899. According to a land acknowledgment statement written by UIUC's Native American House:

> These lands were the lands of the Peoria, Kaskaskia, Piankashaw, Wea, Miami, Mascoutin, Odawa, Sauk, Mesquaki, Kickapoo, Potawatomi, Ojibwe, and Chickasaw Nations. These lands were the traditional territory of these Native Nations prior to their forced removal; these lands continue to carry the stories of these Nations and their struggles for survival and identity.
>
> ("Optional")

This chapter chronicles "Beyond Land Acknowledgement," a performance-installation-arts-based-civic-dialogue created by Dr. Nicole Anderson Cobb, Historian and Playwright, and Latrelle Bright, Teaching Assistant Professor of Theatre, UIUC, during their Spring 2022 three-week residency as part of Allerton's Artist-in-Residence program "Rooting a Deeper Connection." Typically, land acknowledgements are texts read aloud publicly affirming that the lands where individuals are gathered currently were stewarded by Indigenous communities in the past. Land acknowledgements are often an obligatory, yet passive opening to a program that briefly introduces gathered audiences to the Native histories of the land on which they have gathered but fails to provide opportunities for deeper engagement or action.

DOI: 10.4324/9781032636337-20

However, in our "Beyond Land Acknowledgement" program, guests were invited to experience both the presence and erasure of Native histories at Allerton Park & Retreat Center.

We created the "Beyond Land Acknowledgement" performance that evoked 1830s Monticello as a site where Euro-American settlers and Indigenous communities collaborated, clashed, and ceded land rights during the early decades of Illinois's statehood. Monticello was a stop along the 1838 Potawatomi Trail of Death: the forced removal journey of the Potawatomi from Indiana through Illinois, Missouri, Iowa, and into Kansas. Eight hundred and fifty Potawatomi completed the journey and forty-two people died along this trail. In Monticello, two Potawatomi children and two Potawatomi adults died during one of the rest stops along this harrowing journey from Indiana to Kansas.[2] This chapter considers the process of rendering these histories as BIPOC (Black, Indigenous, and People of Color) theatremakers. From the outset, we pursued a series of framing questions that allowed us to explore the shared contours of racial exclusion that marked the histories of this site. As my collaborator Bright has written elsewhere, these questions included:

> What are our (black folks) historical relationships to water and the woods in the United States of America? What hinders black folks from taking advantage of available nature preserves in this region? What is the invitation (or lack thereof) to folks of color in Central Illinois? What is required to access the park? What role must Allerton Park and Retreat Center play in making a safe space for black folks? How do we 'value history' and 'sustain and promote the legacy of Robert Allerton Park' a space, a sanctuary dare we say, for communing with nature in a harried world **<u>and</u>** examine its threads within the fabric of a system that privileged white men and displaced indigenous peoples?
>
> ("Rooting a Deeper Connection")

As someone who has lived as a researcher in various West African, Middle Eastern, and European locales, my experience working at Allerton Park—just 25 miles from my home—was marked by the same dynamics of journeying to a foreign land. Monticello has historically been—and remains—a predominantly white community that exists between my UIUC college town and Allerton Park. Monticello has also had the reputation for being a "sundown town", a town where Blacks could work, but were not allowed to live or own property and needed to depart before nightfall. As a Black woman—who is the descendant of African American Southerners—it has always been ingrained in me to be wary, careful, and aware of spending time in predominantly white spaces, given the history of racial violence experienced by African Americans (historically and into the twenty-first century) who were harmed or killed for being in the wrong place and of the wrong race at the wrong time. Coincidentally, my collaborator Latrelle Bright's mother—also a Southerner—drove to Allerton Park the night before our residency began. Consequently, Bright's mother was deeply concerned about Bright staying in the house alone and asked frequently when I would join her.

Before our arrival, I took all the steps that I would take for overseas research (or as a new Black faculty member on campus) and applied them to my visit to Monticello:

- I contacted stakeholders in advance to provide a letter of introduction and a personal photo, which I asked them to circulate to staff.
- I asked the Allerton staff for identification badges that would associate us with Allerton Park in case either of us was stopped by local police or Allerton staff who didn't know us.
- I asked for clear arrival, check-in, and departure policies and governed myself accordingly.
- I tried to travel to and from Allerton Park during the daytime.
- When we were away from one another, Bright and I also kept each other aware of our schedules, movements, and activities.

Echoing our reservations with respect to the site, some of our invited guests admitted in our post-program discussion that they had begrudgingly attended our event. Others mentioned that they came to Allerton *only* to support us because they have had their own unpleasant experiences with Monticello. Yet another guest mentioned how nervous she was on the drive to Allerton. These comments reflect the challenge of site-specific performance in a location fraught by histories of racial tension and exclusion. From the beginning of our project, we continually contemplated how we could overcome the problematic lore associated with Allerton for guests of color and convince them to accept our invitation to come and experience our work. When we consider the role of the dramaturg with respect to audience engagement, we often focus on the historical context that would enable an audience to fully appreciate a production, but this chapter argues that dramaturgs should also attend to sociocultural barriers to attendance. Thus, the emphasis of this chapter will be offering techniques for framing creative performances occurring in historically fraught sites such that guests of color feel free to engage in an open dialogue that fully considers concerns raised by the locale.

Managing One's Personal History in Fraught Historical Spaces

Before beginning to create theatre, Bright and I found that we had to first process the space ourselves in order to make sense of the histories we were seeking to unravel. Despite the fact that I pursued this opportunity, completed the application process, participated in applicant interviews, and was selected, I still had to process this residency in my body, in the context of my African

American history, and in consideration of my life experience as a historian, researcher, and theatre-maker of color. Consequently, my earliest journal entries emerged as poetry:

"Black Bodies Hanging"

> (4/19/2022)
> Don't worry, silly. (Wink)
> I just meant two sisters hanging out.
> You know
> At Allerton
> On assignment
> Peeling back layers
> Seeking meaning
> To the past
> Under our feet
> I appreciate our caretakers'
> Offer of space
> To allow us to get on one accord
> And yet: the deeper we dig, I suspect the surveillance
> Our own internal surveillance and theirs
> Who ever THEY are will intensify
> Black
> Educated
> Bookish
> Examining
> 50s
> MidLife
> Battle-tested
> Battle-weary
> Carrying our selves
> Our burdens
> The weight of history
> The weight of obligation
> In every encounter
> In this place
> Here we are.
> HERE we are.
> HERE. WE. ARE.

Early journal entries like this one became the source material for our final work. Once we got beyond our initial phase of "processing" the Allerton campus ourselves, we spent the first week of our residency researching the campus and local histories, the second week preparing for the installation and performance, and the final week expanding our research and hosting a community open mic.

Creating the Performance and Cultivating an Audience

We knew that in order to invite a diverse group of guests to attend our event, we had to be intentional about how we crafted the invitation and constructed the program itself:

- We curated a guest list of 30 to 40 individuals—including many K-12 and university educators—who would be receptive to our invitation. Knowing we would be inviting an audience dominated by people of color, it was important for us to create a space where the white gaze did not dominate the experience.
- We kept the number of invited guests small to cultivate an intimate experience.
- We sent guests an introductory letter that provided logistical information (including our personal phone numbers) and multiple sets of directions to access our location from various directions.
- In the letter, we provided guidance on attire and suggested items guests should bring with them. We also included a disclaimer for all attendees warning them "that sensitive topics of colonial occupation, Native American removal, and settler-Indigenous conquest-related violence will be discussed and depicted" so they could discern whether or not the topics would be acceptable for themselves and their children.
- We included a meal understanding that—for most communities—breaking bread together helps establish common ground and lubricates discussion across differences and about challenging topics.
- We asked permission to share guest information with one another for those who wanted to carpool so individuals did not have to travel alone.
- We constructed a playlist and reflection questions for attendees to consider as they drove to and from Allerton to allow them to treat the drive as part of the experience.
- We made sure we had clear signage, as The Brick House is a more remote location of Allerton Park that many had never visited, and few even knew existed.
- We sent a post-program evaluation soliciting feedback on logistics, program content, and suggested improvements for future presentations.

The program proceeded as follows:

- 1:45–2:00: Gathering and Greetings at the Barn and Community Stroll Over to The Brick House
- 2:00: *Call to "Settle In" Performance on Front Porch*
  - "Settle In" was an opening monologue offered on the porch of The Brick House by my collaborator Latrelle Bright as attendees stood among a field of over 350 flags planted on the lawn. Each flag represented one

Figure 16.1 350 Flags in front of The Brick House Campus, Allerton Park & Retreat Center, May 1, 2022. Photo by Christopher Fuller, Christopher Fuller Photography.

of the hundreds of treaties broken with Indigenous nations throughout American history (Figure 16.1). We then provided a preview for the experience inside the house.

- 2:00–2:30: Exploring the Rooms: "The Settle In," "The Indigenous Room," "The Settler Room," and "The Contemporary Room"
    - Three rooms on the ground floor of The Brick House were transformed into installations, each examining a different aspect of Indigenous-settler relations. As attendees explored the space, singer J'Lyn Hope (our residency musician) offered bluesy renditions of American standards such as "America, The Beautiful" and negro spirituals. It was crucial for us to decenter the settler narrative, so we required attendees to visit the Native/Indigenous history-themed room first, featuring the histories of communities indigenous to pre-Allerton Monticello. Then, the attendees moved into "The Settler Room" to take in information, timelines, and activities related to the settler-Indigenous conflict (Figure 16.2). In this room, we also erected a symbolic grave to honor the memories of the four Potawatomi who died in Monticello as they were forcibly marched through in September 1838. Following this makeshift memorial, my daughter and I presented a dramatic reading from settler journals and letters, reflecting on settler-Indigenous relations during the mid-nineteenth century.

Figure 16.2 "Beyond Land Acknowledgement" installation visitors in The Settler Room, The Brick House Campus, Allerton Park & Retreat Center, May 1, 2022. Photo by Christopher Fuller, Christopher Fuller Photography.

- 2:30–2:45: Break and Refreshments
- 2:45–3:30: *Beyond Land Acknowledgements Call and Response*
    - In "The Contemporary Room," attendees had refreshments, and we led a discussion about the installation, contemporary debates about historicizing this land, historical erasure, the historical research that informed our performances, including these histories in K-12 education curricula, and continuing this work in other contexts.
- 3:30–4:00: Thanks and Closing

Takeaways from Our Time as Artists-in-Residence at Allerton Park

The histories that we dramatized could be touched, handled, and walked on. They were torn from books, papering the walls, heard in song wafting through the space, and hanging from ceilings. Here, history could be literally grappled with as audience-participants brushed against timelines, documents, and artifacts, listening, feeling, and reflecting. Thus, this creative, tactile, performative approach provided a way of accessing history distinct from most museum or public installations.

Additionally, inviting the children in our lives to attend and help to curate the exhibit gave children the opportunity to invest in their own history as young Central Illinoisans. Children were invited to make posters, take photos, write on banners, and read aloud as part of the program. Jump rope, swings, and games on the lawn provided opportunities for kinesthetic learning as well.

Finally, what was most potent and valuable about this experience was the opportunity to listen to audiences lament that this history is not taught more broadly, marvel at our process from research to performance, and be inspired to connect this history with aspects of their own life and work as educators.

Exercise

When planning a site-specific piece that animates fraught histories, reflect on the following considerations:

1. What do you need to do to prepare yourself financially, logistically, materially, and emotionally for this project?
2. What obstacles do you foresee for your collaborators to mount the production? How might your collaborators' identities (race, gender, sexuality, class, and disability, among others) affect their ability to comfortably access the site and the stories being told? What protocols need to be in place to better facilitate their involvement?
3. What obstacles do you foresee for your targeted audiences to support this production? How might your audiences' identities affect their ability to comfortably access the site and the stories being told? What protocols need to be in place to better facilitate their attendance and engagement?

Notes

1 See https://allerton.illinois.edu.

2 For more information on the Potawatomi Trail of Death (1838), visit the Potawatomi Trail of Death Association's website: http://www.potawatomi-tda.org.

Works Cited

Bright, Latrelle. "Rooting a Deeper Connection: Allerton Artist-In-Residence." *Latrelle Bright: Theatre Maker*. https://latrellebright.com/projects/the-arachne-project/rooting-a-deeper-connection-allerton-artist-in-residence/.

Hammie, Jessica. "Nicole Anderson Cobb and Latrelle Bright Ask: What Has Grown on Stolen Land?" *Smile Politely Magazine*, 4 May 2022, https://www.smilepolitely.com/arts/nicole_anderson-cobb_and_latrelle_bright_ask_what_has_grown_on_stolen_land/. Accessed 19 April 2023.

Hammie, Jessica. "Rooting Deeper with Nicole Anderson Cobb and Latrelle Bright." *Sixty Inches from Center Magazine*, 1 August 2022, https://sixtyinchesfromcenter.org/rooting-deeper-with-nicole-anderson-cobb-and-latrelle-bright/. Accessed 10 April 2023.

Holtz, Maureen. *Robert Allerton: His Parks and Legacies*. Arcadia Publishing, 2021.

UIUC Native American House. "Optional Land Acknowledgement Statement suggested by Native American House (for on-campus events)." *University of Illinois-Urbana-Champaign Office of the Chancellor*. https://chancellor.illinois.edu/land_acknowledgement.html.

17 A Public Historian's Guide to Dramaturging Native Plays

Laurie Arnold

Cherokee playwright Mary Kathryn Nagle has a message for theatres reluctant to produce Native plays because they fear making mistakes: "You will. I make mistakes every day. But that's not the point…Native stories will give you something powerful, something healing—if you listen" ("Native Voices"). Staging meaningful and legitimate productions of Native stories requires research beyond the standard practice. Dramaturgs and productions must be informed by Native perspectives and tribally-authored materials. Native playwrights are Indigenizing theatre; dramaturgs share in this work when they center Native voices from the past and the present. Archives contain multitudes, but most of the content is *about* Native people not *by* Native people, which makes them valuable but incomplete sources of information.

This chapter offers guidance on how dramaturgs can use archives to achieve culturally meaningful and ethical approaches to producing Native plays and plays that feature Native storylines. Using *Off the Rails* by Randy Reinholz (Choctaw) as a case study for recognizing the presence of Native stories, I will explore how documentary research and content written by tribes can animate those stories. The chapter also presents adaptable best practices for inviting tribes into collaboration and consultation on productions of plays about their communities. I approach dramaturgy through my practice as a historian and my lived experience as a Native person. These contexts inform this chapter.

Rails premiered at the Oregon Shakespeare Festival in July 2017; more than 27,000 people saw the show during its run. The setting is Genoa, Nebraska, in the 1880s. The action takes place in a brothel, a military fort, and a US Indian boarding school. Native characters (in roles performed by Native actors) populate the play, along with a few non-Native characters. An adaptation of Shakespeare's *Measure for Measure*, *Rails* tells the story of Momaday, a young Pawnee man sentenced to death for marrying an Irish immigrant, and his sister Isabel, who tries to save him while also thwarting the corrupt and sexually violent Army captain of the fort where Momaday is imprisoned. As characters move through the historical settings, they illustrate failure—failure of US policies designed to erase Native people and their cultures. *Rails*

DOI: 10.4324/9781032636337-21

demonstrates how, instead of vanishing, Native people asserted agency and strategy in various ways as they responded to federal Indian policies. The settings in the play are well represented in academic scholarship, library collections, and tribal sources, offering many entry points for dramaturgs.

When staging or researching Native plays, dramaturgs and theatres must recognize the political and cultural distinctiveness between tribes rather than imagining a generalized "Native American" story. Tribes are self-governing nations—there are currently 574 federally recognized tribes in the United States—and must be represented as such on stage. In *Off the Rails*, Momaday and Isabel are Pawnee, and Momaday speaks Pawnee at various points in the play. Another character, Alexie, is Kiowa, and he, too, uses his Indigenous language in some of his dialogue. Speaking about boarding schools and education, Isabel laments how little the US government knows or cares about Native people: "They don't know our nations. To them, we are not Kiowa, Lakota, or Pawnee—just Indians" (1.6).

Tribal websites and associated resources will provide a strong foundation for dramaturgs. Both the Pawnee Nation and the Kiowa Tribe operate their own government websites ("Pawnee Nation"; "KiowaTribe"). The Pawnee site offers narratives about their history and culture, as well as details about government operations. The Kiowa Tribe's site is geared more toward tribal operations and contains less historical and cultural content, but the Oklahoma Historical Society has a strong encyclopedia entry about Kiowa history (Kracht).

Regional historical societies often produce well-researched histories about adjacent tribal nations, and more museums and historical societies are creating historical narratives in collaboration with local tribes. Tribes increasingly cooperate with arts organizations, museums, and academics interested in sharing interpretive space; they may also be interested in similar shared work with theatres. Scholars and interpretive professionals often want to initiate their research by contacting tribes. It is better instead to conduct as much research as possible—through tribal websites and in academic scholarship—before contacting a Tribal Historic Preservation Office, for example. This practice demonstrates a serious commitment to learning. It is also important to ask tribes whether the production may use content from their websites. We are used to considering information on the internet as public, and certainly, tribal websites are intentionally public-facing. However, best practice conduct means contacting a tribe to share news of the production and how you've learned from their content, as well as inviting them into conversation about the work. Some tribes may engage, and some may not; the effort to include them matters and demonstrates respect for their nation and their history, as well as for contemporary tribal citizens and priorities.

Respect is particularly important when staging narratives that include trauma. *Rails* addresses federal Indian boarding schools; other productions, such as Nagle's *Sovereignty*, offer first-person tribal accounts of land theft and violence committed against Cherokee citizens during Indian removal. Native American playwrights offer new interpretations of the past in their work, and theatres can partner in Indigenizing American history when they produce plays like Reinholz's and Nagle's. Staging these works carries unique responsibilities to living communities, to telling the stories ethically, accurately, and respectfully.

The boarding school featured in *Rails* was an actual federal boarding school. The Indian Industrial School in Genoa, Nebraska, operated from 1884 to 1934 and was the fourth-largest non-reservation Indian boarding school. Indian agents and other federal officials often forcibly removed children from their homes to "enroll" them in school. The school was constructed on former Pawnee reservation lands, lands the tribe ceded in a series of treaties with the United States. When Nebraska became a state and joined the Union, the state nullified tribal rights to their reservation, sold the land, and used the proceeds to purchase land for the Pawnee in Oklahoma which has become home for the Pawnee Nation ("Pawnee Nation"). It is possible to visit the Genoa Industrial School site and museum; the Genoa U.S. Indian School Foundation operates a website and offers both virtual and in-person tours during specific months ("Genoa Indian School").

While visiting physical historic sites is ideal, it is not always possible. As dramaturgs conduct historical research, online resources about Carlisle Indian School and its students will be more accessible than Genoa or other institutions. The school, in Carlisle, Pennsylvania, was established in 1879 and is perhaps the most well-known boarding school, in large part because its founder Captain Richard Henry Pratt summarized his educational assimilationist goals as "kill the Indian, save the man" (46). In 2013, Dickinson College in Pennsylvania created a searchable database of materials related to Carlisle and its students and initiated an ongoing digitization project of materials held at the Washington D.C. branch of the National Archives and Records Administration and beyond ("Carlisle Indian").

The database has robust collections of student records, including demographic information such as age, gender, and tribe, as well as photographs and documents related to the school's administration and more. If a dramaturg were interested in developing their comprehension about Pawnee students' lives at a boarding school, they could search within Pawnee student records to understand where a student's family lived and in what type of home, if they had siblings, what kind of life they imagined for themselves after returning home, and so on. In the collection's "before" photos, dramaturgs can observe material culture items from students' communities, possessions they might have arrived with at school, and their attire. In some cases, it is clear that families dressed children in their best clothing and made sure children were accompanied by treasured items. Historian David Wallace Adams shared a Hopi student's story as a poignant example of ways Native children experienced these schools. Prior to the student's departure for an Indian boarding school in Arizona, the boy's grandfather wove him a very fine blanket and sent it to school with him. The school took it from him upon his arrival, along with his clothes and other belongings. As an adult, he recalled the blanket and its loss: later that academic year, he saw the schoolmaster's wife using it for herself (Adams 343). Native families and children were told to trust the United States and put their faith in education. While only one incident, this story is emblematic of the small ways the United States betrayed that trust, an action we now understand as part of a much larger story of betrayal and abuse.

For dramaturgs, Dickinson's searchable online database is a boon, especially because images of documents are posted with each entry. Digitizing these materials has, in some ways, allowed families and communities to be reunited with the children they lost generations ago. At the same time, the public availability of these records has distressed some families, who wonder why their ancestors' privacy isn't protected and why efforts weren't made to contact families prior to publication of the documents. Productions and dramaturgs who employ these materials must remain sensitive to the reality that the individuals named in the documents and presented in photographs were living people, members of families, and that some children never returned home from boarding schools. It is important to care for the people and the materials in this context and for dramaturgs to be vigilant about their responsible use in the public arena of the theatre.

Native American and First Nations boarding schools have captured the public imagination in recent years, in part due to discoveries that children's remains—whom communities refer to as ancestors—still reside on current and former boarding school sites. In 2021, United States Interior Secretary Deb Haaland (Laguna Pueblo) announced the creation of the Federal Indian Boarding School Initiative, an effort to gather data about the more-than-400 federal Indian boarding schools in order to ultimately "address the inter-generational impact of Indian boarding schools to shed light on the unspoken traumas of the past" ("BIA"). The Interior Department recognizes family and community concerns about how information collected will be used and by whom. Principal Deputy Assistant Secretary for Indian Affairs Bryan Newland (Bay Mills Ojibwe) noted, "We will engage in Tribal consultation on how best to use this information, protect burial sites, and respect families and communities" ("BIA"). As producers consider staging *Off the Rails* and other Native plays, it is critically important that they comprehend US assimilative goals, the intent behind separating children from families and communities, and the ongoing trauma from those lost years and lost children and that they work with dramaturgs to help audiences understand this context and see the deeper narratives of the play. Not every Native play has historical themes, but US Indian policies continue to impact contemporary Native lives, in tangible ways ranging from land ownership to legal jurisdiction. The more dramaturgs can develop their knowledge of nineteenth-century Native histories, the more successful they will be in representing the Native American past as well as the present.

Producing Native plays rich with historical content offers opportunities to both make Native lives more visible and recall how linguistically vibrant North America used to be. Maintaining strong trade and kinship ties among tribes required multilingualism; English only became dominant because of boarding schools. To complement tribal language revitalization efforts, contemporary Native American playwrights often use Indigenous languages in their plays and invite speakers and tribal language programs into conversations about phrases, dialogue, and meaning. *Off the Rails* employed these practices when it included Pawnee and Kiowa at central moments in the narrative. Improperly speaking Indigenous languages may be among the mistakes theatres fear they will make, but the Pawnee Nation and the Kiowa Tribe have made language materials, including lessons and pronunciation, available on their websites. As dramaturgs seek to identify appropriate pronunciation and create a glossary with accurate translations, these kinds of resources will be invaluable and will offer meaningful opportunities to connect productions with tribal cultural sovereignty priorities.

During the last twenty years, Native artists have built a formidable network for creators, fostering growth across storytelling formats from coast to coast. Native stories are here to stay, and the breadth in representation across regions, genres, and narratives presents dynamism audiences are only beginning to recognize. Theaters must produce this work, and they must do it well. In a discussion about contemporary storytelling, Sicangu Lakota playwright Larissa FastHorse cautioned against remaining focused on tropes of tragedy. She characterized these narratives as voyeurism; they also maroon Native people within historical stereotypes (McDermott). Archival sources, particularly those created in the nineteenth and early twentieth centuries, can reinforce tragedy and hopelessness; they underestimate and undervalue Native people. Dramaturgs are well positioned to partner in expanding historical narratives and telling stories in a good way. Collaborations between playwrights, dramaturgs, and tribes can redefine standard practices for theatres and amplify the chorus of Native voices asserting "we are still here!"

Exercise

Two federal repositories hold hundreds of millions of documents and images about Native Americans: the Library of Congress and the National Archives and Records Administration (NARA). The National Congress of American Indians (NCAI) is the largest intertribal Native rights organization in the United States. *Indian Country Today* is a nonprofit digital news source about the Indigenous world, led by and staffed by Native journalists. Dramaturgs researching specific tribal communities—whether to support productions treating Native histories or to provide fuller local historical context to a production—should begin with tribal nation websites. The next step in their research should include a visit to any of these resources and conducting a keyword search. This process prioritizes tribally created content and leverages archival collections to reinscribe Native narratives on American stages.

Works Cited

Adams, David Wallace. "Schooling the Hopi: Federal Indian Policy Writ Small, 1887–1917." *Pacific Historical Review* vol. 48, no. 3, 1979, pp. 335–56.

"About Us." *Genoa U.S. Indian School Foundation Museum*, n.d. https://genoaindianschoolmuseum.org/. Accessed 18 February 2023.

"Home." *Carlisle Indian School Digital Resource Center*, n.d. https://carlisleindian.dickinson.edu/. Accessed 18 February 2023.

"Home." *Pawnee Nation*, n.d. https://pawneenation.org/. Accessed 20 February 2023.

Indian Country Today. https://ictnews.org/. Accessed 4 August 2023.

Kracht, Benjamin R. "Kiowa." *The Encyclopedia of Oklahoma History and Culture*, n.d. https://www.okhistory.org/publications/enc/entry.php?entry=KI017. Accessed 16 January 2023.

"K'YAKHOME BAH AH HEI-DAE." *Kiowa Tribe*, n.d. https://www.kiowatribe.org/. Accessed 20 February 2023.

Library of Congress. https://www.loc.gov/. Accessed 4 August 2023.

McDermott, Jim. "'My Tone Is Indigenous': Larissa FastHorse on Native Comedy and Storytelling." *American Theatre*, 14 April 2023, https://www.americantheatre.org/2023/04/14/my-tone-is-indigenous-larissa-fasthorse-on-native-comedy-and-storytelling/. Accessed 14 April 2023.

Nagle, Mary Kathryn. "Native Voices on the American Stage." *Howl Round Theatre Commons*, 22 February 2015, https://howlround.com/native-voices-american-stage. Accessed 13 January 2023.

National Archives and Records Administration. https://www.archives.gov/. Accessed 4 August 2023.

National Congress of American Indians. https://www.ncai.org/. Accessed 4 August 2023.

Pratt, Richard Henry. "Proceedings of the National Conference of Charities and Correction," *Hathi Trust*, 23 June 1892, https://babel.hathitrust.org/cgi/pt?id=wu.89030648919&view=1up&seq=11. Accessed 18 February 2023.

Reinholz, Randy. *Off the Rails*. 2017.

U.S. Department of the Interior. "Secretary Haaland Announces Federal Indian Boarding School Initiative," *Bureau of Indian Affairs*, 22 June 2021, https://www.bia.gov/service/federal-indian-boarding-school-initiative. Accessed 23 January 2023.

18 Archiving AfroLatine Theatre

Daphnie Sicre

In 2007, as I embarked on my dissertation on AfroLatine theatre,[1] the absence of accessible archives on AfroLatinidad and theatre prompted me to undertake the creation of a scholarly archive to support my research. This academic pursuit posed distinctive challenges throughout both the dissertation process and subsequent publication endeavors. My research addressed a subject matter that had rarely been explored, and as a result, I found myself quoting my own work in academic papers. Adding to the complexity of lacking an established formal archive, language barriers have further complicated my publication process, with editors resorting to Google Translate for corrections and requesting translations of plays with Spanish titles that lack official English versions. These experiences are a testament to the historical marginalization of AfroLatine voices and the scarcity of available archival material.

The creation of an AfroLatine archive for US theatrical productions has proven to be a significant undertaking. While some Latine theatre creatives and organizations have begun archiving Latine work, archives focused exclusively on AfroLatine productions remain scarce. This effort is crucial, given the historical underrepresentation of AfroLatine productions, which has only recently begun to gain attention in the American theatre. Chronic underfunding has further complicated this task. Without resources in place to ensure the long-term preservation of its histories, this integral aspect of Latine theatrical performance is at risk of remaining underdocumented. This chapter offers a practical window into my step-by-step process of creating an AfroLatine performance archive, highlighting best dramaturgical practices for creating such an archive. Dramaturgs, particularly those associated with theatre companies, are well positioned to contribute to performance/theatre archives. The chapter explores what aspiring performance archivists, dramaturgs, and scholars should know when documenting historically marginalized artists and outlines the role of dramaturgs in building similar resources. It aims to foster a deeper understanding of the crucial work required to preserve and amplify the voices of historically marginalized theatre artists.

DOI: 10.4324/9781032636337-22

Why Is It Important to Archive AfroLatine Theatre?

The Latinx Theatre Commons (LTC) recently applied for a unique Wallace Foundation grant to research and document the living history of Latinx theatre in the United States, aiming to create an interactive map of existing archives. This initiative addresses the lack of continuity in archiving Latinx theatre. Chronic underfunding has hindered the institutionalization of independent projects, leading to reliance on partnerships. Notable efforts include The LA Latinx Theatre Oral History project, The Cuban Theater Digital Archive, El Teatro Campesino Archives, Latino Theater Initiative/Center Theater Group Records, and the Fornés Institute by LTC. Café Onda on *HowlRound* served as an LTC platform for publishing blogs, essays, and interviews, with vivid event archiving. Brian Herrera, Trevor Boffone, Carla Della Gatta, Jorge Huerta, and Lillian Manzor have contributed individual archives to Latine theatre. Despite these existing archives, much of Latinx theatre history resides in the memories of those involved.

While Latine theatre history is partially documented through various means, there remains a notable void when it comes to AfroLatinidad or Afro-Latine performance in the United States. Monolithic notions of Latinidad often fail to recognize racial differences under that umbrella term. Too often, Black Latine communities are not represented in Latine theatre. This omission perpetuates the marginalization of AfroLatine voices and narratives within the broader discourse on Latine theatre. Although this has slowly begun to change, we still have a long way to go. Creating an archive specifically dedicated to AfroLatine theatre is of the utmost importance to rectify the historical and ongoing underrepresentation of this vital aspect of Latine theatrical performance.

Creating an Archive of AfroLatine Theatre

As a result, my aforementioned experiences of forging a scholarly path for myself working with informal collections, I decided to create an archive. I partnered with Nicole Murph, Reference and Instruction Librarian at William H. Hannon Library at Loyola Marymount University to create an exhibit: "AfroLatines in Los Angeles: Unveiling Voices, Empowering Communities." This exhibition not only marked the celebration of AfroLatinidad but also represented a significant effort to illuminate the often obscured history and remarkable contributions of AfroLatines in Los Angeles. It was also the first exhibit on AfroLatinidad the university had ever done. The exhibit focused on Afro-Mexicans' experiences, achievements, and struggles in Los Angeles, the United States, and Mexico, and on the United States' relationship to Central and South America and the Caribbean. As part of the exhibit, we curated two panels: "Empowering AfroLatines in Los Angeles: Uplifting Communities" and "AfroLatine Theatre Artists." The latter panel delved into the world of AfroLatine theatre artists in the Los Angeles community whose creativity has not only shaped the local theatre scene but also provided a powerful voice for marginalized communities. From the exhibit, we created a LibGuide that not only focuses on AfroLatines in Los Angeles but also includes a whole subcategory dedicated to AfroLatine theatre. By collecting and curating materials related to AfroLatine playwrights, productions, and cultural contributions, the archive provides a wide-reaching platform for AfroLatine communities to share their work. Since it was created as a Library Guide, the archive has become a public repository that safeguards AfroLatine theatre history for current and future generations, making it accessible to anyone with internet access. This archive has become an essential tool for academic research, artistic inspiration, and community empowerment, fostering a deeper understanding and appreciation of the AfroLatine experience in the United States.

The above experience offers a starting point for dramaturgs who wish to collaborate with libraries to build resources that enrich our understanding of underrepresented narratives in the performing arts. By actively participating in documenting and preserving historically marginalized artists' contributions, dramaturgs can advocate for equity and representation in the performing arts. The archives they contribute to can foster a more comprehensive understanding of the multifaceted experiences within the theatre community. As dramaturgs contribute to creating such resources, they actively shape the narrative of the performing arts, ensuring diverse stories become integral components of the broader discourse. Establishing an archive dedicated to AfroLatine Theatre stands as a crucial endeavor for rectifying historical erasures and amplifying marginalized voices. However, the journey has been significantly influenced by considerations of funding and accessibility, which have shaped decisions and processes related to the archive.

Funding and Accessibility

The ongoing struggle for funding has significantly impacted my ability to realize this documentation of AfroLatine theatrical histories, particularly as I have undertaken this labor without compensation. Securing grants for individual or grassroots initiatives such as this one proves difficult, as traditional funding sources may not fully grasp the importance of preserving marginalized histories; their subsequent failure to support this work has the potential to limit the archive's reach. Individual funding efforts have played a critical role in supporting scholars and archivists dedicated to preserving and recording Latine performance, sending a powerful message about the value of Latine theatre, and especially AfroLatine theatre.

Beyond funding, maintaining accessibility to archives adds complexity to the creation process. Creating an archive attached to a library helps alleviate financial constraints because the archive can rely on the institution's existing infrastructure. Access to a resource librarian, basic web design, and long-term web page hosting eliminates significant barriers to the creation of the archive. Moreover, developing the archive as an online resource expands its reach. Even so, unique challenges arise when the archive is managed by an individual, especially in the absence of a centralized physical location for the archive or a dedicated host institution.

Further Challenges in Creating an Archive

Dependency on the Archivist and Getting Outside Organizations/ Publications to Acknowledge These Archives

As the sole archivist, I bear the significant responsibility of preserving and disseminating knowledge about AfroLatine theatre and have become a go-to resource for researchers seeking information on these performances. Handling inquiries and ensuring continued accessibility are daunting tasks that underscore the multifaceted challenges associated with gaining recognition as an archive. Proactive efforts are essential to elevating visibility and credibility. Scholarly collaborations, such as my partnership with my university's library, serve as cross-referencing points of validation. Additionally, collaborations with external entities, like *HowlRound*, amplify impact and garner wider acknowledgment of the importance and urgency of this work from organizations and publications. For instance, I curated an eight-week session with AfroLatine Playwrights for *HowlRound*, "a free and open platform for theatremakers worldwide that amplifies progressive and disruptive ideas about [theatre] and facilitates connections between diverse practitioners" (Emerson College). It serves as an open-access resource, increasing the visibility of AfroLatine theatre and the archive. Further, the financial support provided by *HowlRound* and the university advanced the archive's goals by funding the artists involved. *HowlRound* paid the eight playwrights I invited to lead sessions, and the university paid the AfroLatine panelists who came to talk to students. This external backing provided necessary resources and institutional legitimacy, allowing the archive to thrive in its mission of preserving and elevating the rich heritage of AfroLatine theatre, while also remaining accessible.

Limited Visibility and Reach

Without a dedicated physical space or an institutionalized archive, the visibility and reach of the archive may be limited, resulting in researchers and scholars not discovering and utilizing this resource. This lack of visibility might also hinder efforts to collaborate or share findings with other dramaturgs, archivists, scholars, or organizations in the field. Scholarly collaborations play a crucial role in elevating the visibility and credibility of an archive. Publishing in academic journals and scholarly collections allows for the dissemination of findings and the demonstration of the archive's value and the curator's expertise. Participation in academic and artistic conferences, panel discussions, and workshops further enhances visibility, showcasing the depth and importance of the collected materials. Once an archive is established, I also urge dramaturgs and curators to engage in partnerships with other dramaturgs, researchers, archivists, and scholars in the field, so that the archive becomes part of a broader network of knowledge exchange. My next step in creating my archive will be to gather further contributions from scholars who are already working to preserve Latine theatre, particularly where they may be working on something new that I have not already referenced.[2]

Sustainability Concerns

Ensuring the longevity of an archive is crucial, especially when the person or organization responsible for it can no longer maintain it, risking the loss of valuable cultural heritage. Establishing a clear succession plan is essential for continuity, involving the identification and training of individuals or institutions to assume responsibility for preserving the archive. Without proper planning, there is a danger of erasing historical contributions and losing significant cultural heritage. I currently lack a succession plan for my AfroLatine theatre archive. While the library guide stays with Loyola Marymount, if I leave my institution, my hope is that writings like this chapter and the existence of the archive will inspire new scholars and dramaturgs to continue this work.[3] I want to encourage dramaturgs particularly to contribute to these efforts, recognizing that they often already maintain important documentation of productions as they are underway, which could provide unique insights into the performance practices of marginalized theatre artists.

Potential Bias or Limitations

While I have a huge passion for archiving AfroLatine theatre and folks appreciate all that I do, as an individual, I might inadvertently bring personal biases or limitations to the archive. Without the collective input and diverse perspectives that institutional archives often offer, there is a risk of certain voices or experiences being over- or underrepresented. Addressing these challenges requires collaborative efforts from the broader theatre community to recognize and support archivists. Again, establishing partnerships with universities, theatres, and cultural institutions could help ensure the longevity and accessibility of the archive, as well as counter any possible bias. Additionally, working directly with artists to ensure that their work is represented according to their wishes can be beneficial in addressing the potential limitations and misrepresentations associated with archival practice.

Despite challenges, my goal is to contribute to the establishment of an AfroLatine theatre archive, ensuring its growth, preserving a rich history of artistic expressions, and serving as a visible and invaluable resource. This archive plays a crucial role in safeguarding the history of AfroLatine theatrical performance, contributing to a deeper and indispensable understanding of AfroLatine experiences in the United States.

Exercise

Take an active step toward preserving AfroLatine theatre history.

1. Identify three key artists or productions that have significantly contributed to the AfroLatine theatrical landscape. Do not consult the resources that I have created. Note where you found information about these artists or productions. How robust were these sources? Did you have to consult multiple sources?
2. Turn to the "AfroLatine in Theatre" LibGuide and the "AfroLatine Superfriends Playwriting Hour" on *HowlRound* (cited below). How do these resources deepen your understanding of the artists and productions you identified above, if only to provide further context?
3. Consider how you can contribute to building visibility for your identified artists and productions.

Notes

1. Sicre, Daphnie. *American Sangre: An Exploration of Afro-Latin@ Representation in the Play* Platanos y Collard Greens. 2017. New York University, PhD dissertation.
2. In addition to the Latine theatre scholars cited above, this includes Florencia Cornet, Patricia Herrera, Jade Power-Sotomayor, and Olga Sanchez-Saltveit.
3. Since writing this chapter, I no longer work at Loyola Marymount, and Nicole Murphy will keep the archive active but I will no longer contribute to it, as LMU is no longer my institution.

Works Cited

"AfroLatine Superfriends Playwriting Hour." Edited by Daphnie Sicre, *HowlRound Theatre Commons*, https://howlround.com/series/afrolatine-superfriends-playwriting-hour. Accessed 31 July 2023.

Boffone, Trevor. "'A Home Page for All of Us': A History of *Café Onda: Journal of the Latinx Theatre Commons* (2013–2018)." *Latin American Theatre Review*, vol. 54, no. 2, 2021, pp. 237–49. *Project MUSE*, doi: 10.1353/ltr.2021.0013.

Emerson College. "HowlRound." *Office of the Arts*. https://emerson.edu/departments/office-arts/howlround.

Sicre, Daphnie. "AfroLatine in Theatre." Loyola Marymount University. https://libguides.lmu.edu/AfroLatinesLosAngeles.

Sicre, Daphnie. "Afro-Latinx Themes in Theatre Today." *The Routledge Companion to African American Theatre and Performance*, edited by Kathy A. Perkins, Sandra L. Richards, Renée Alexander Craft, and Thomas F. DeFrantz. Routledge, 2019, pp. 272–277.

Sicre, Daphnie. "AfroLatinidad: Being Black and Latinx in Theatre Today." *Theatre Symposium: Theatre and Race*. Guest Editor Andy Gibb, vol. 29. March 2022, pp. 49–63.

Sicre, Daphnie. "Discussing Intersectionality of AfroLatinidad in Entertainment and Performance." *The Routledge Companion to Latinx Theatre and Performance*, edited by Noe Montez and Olga Sanchez Saltveit. Routledge, 2024.

Sicre, Daphnie. "'Marimacha' Laughs Its Way through Representation of Latine, Black, and Queer Characters." *HowlRound Theatre Commons*, https://howlround.com/marimacha-laughs-its-way-through-representation-latine-black-and-queer-characters. Accessed 31 July 2023.

Index

For Product Safety Concerns and Information please contact our EU representative GPSR@taylorandfrancis.com
Taylor & Francis Verlag GmbH, Kaufingerstraße 24, 80331 München, Germany

www.ingramcontent.com/pod-product-compliance
Lightning Source LLC
LaVergne TN
LVHW010921110826
845149LV00013B/2438

* 9 7 8 1 0 3 2 6 3 6 2 9 0 *